WALKING IN NORFOLK

WALKING IN NORFOLK

by Laurence Mitchell

JUNIPER HOUSE, MURLEY MOSS,
OXENHOLME ROAD, KENDAL, CUMBRIA LA9 7RL
www.cicerone.co.uk

© Laurence Mitchell 2017
Second edition 2017
ISBN: 978 1 85284 869 9
Reprinted 2020 (with updates) and 2021
First edition 2013

Printed in China on responsibly sourced paper on behalf of Latitude Press Ltd.
A catalogue record for this book is available from the British Library.

Acknowledgements

Thanks to David Vince and Nicola Draycott for their helpful advice on some of these walks.

Updates to this Guide

While every effort is made by our authors to ensure the accuracy of guidebooks as they go to print, changes can occur during the lifetime of an edition. Any updates that we know of for this guide will be on the Cicerone website (www.cicerone.co.uk/869/updates), so please check before planning your trip. We also advise that you check information about such things as transport, accommodation and shops locally. Even rights of way can be altered over time. We are always grateful for information about any discrepancies between a guidebook and the facts on the ground, sent by email to updates@cicerone.co.uk or by post to Cicerone, Juniper House, Murley Moss, Oxenholme Road, Kendal, LA9 7RL.

Register your book: To sign up to receive free updates, special offers and GPX files where available, register your book at www.cicerone.co.uk.

Front cover: A sunny ride in Thetford Forest (Walk 31)

CONTENTS

Route symbols on OS map extracts
(for OS legend see printed OS maps)

 route

(🛉) start/finish point

◄ route direction

alt route

OS map extracts reproduced at 1:40,000 (2.5cm to 1km)

Features on the overview map

———— County/Unitary boundary

National Park

Urban area

Area of Outstanding Natural Beauty

Boat in the Morston Salt Marshes at Blakeney (Walk 24)

Round tower church, commonly found in Norfolk, at Burgh Castle near Great Yarmouth (Walk 11)

INTRODUCTION

A rich harvest – straw bales in the fields just outside North Walsham (Walk 3)

'Very flat, Norfolk', asserts Amanda in Noël Coward's *Private Lives*, reflecting pretty much the commonly held view of the county: a place, with attitude perhaps (think of its heroes – Horatio Nelson, Thomas Paine, Delia Smith, Stephen Fry...Alan Partridge), but certainly not with altitude. The stereotyped view, although misleading, is understandable enough, as most people have some sort of image of Norfolk even if they have never visited the county. Many will have seen the vast sandy expanse of North Norfolk's Holkham Beach in films like *Shakespeare in Love* or TV programmes like Stephen Fry's *Kingdom*. Many more will think of boating holidays on the Norfolk Broads, or

make associations with the low-lying Fenland region of the far west of the county: aspects of Norfolk, certainly, but not the full picture by any means.

While it is undeniable that the Fenland region of the county's far west is flat and low-lying, as are the marshes and waterways of the Broads in the east, between these two extremes there is a great deal of topography going on. The fact is, Norfolk is far more varied than most outsiders imagine, with several distinct types of landscape, some of which are unique to the county. In addition to the shimmering water-world of the Broads, and the black soil and arrow-straight channels of the Fens (actually, just a small fraction of the county's landscape),

Old Hunstanton is popular for its beach and its very distinctive cliffs

Norfolk also has the sandy Brecks, rolling pastoral farmland, ancient woodland, meandering rivers and, the jewel in the crown, the gorgeous North Norfolk coast with its beaches, shingle banks, salt marshes and tidal mud flats. There are few other counties in southern England – or anywhere in the United Kingdom for that matter – that have quite as much sheer variety within their boundaries.

Of course, topography is not the be-all and end-all of a landscape's beauty. As any fan of the Fens will tell you, what the landscape lacks in elevation it makes up for with enormous skies and cloud formations of Himalayan proportions. Indeed, I have been told – quite seriously – by a native Norfolk acquaintance that 'The trouble with mountains is that they get in the way of the view'. Although I do not subscribe to that view myself, after decades living in East Anglia I have at least come round to thinking that even the most diffidently undulating landscapes have plenty to offer in their own right.

The joy of walking in Norfolk is to experience this variety of landscapes in the raw – to follow the course of a river upstream, to walk along ancient footpaths, to stumble upon pristine tracts of woodland that have been around since the last Ice Age and villages that were thriving at the time of the Domesday Book, before the Norman invasion dramatically changed the look of the countryside. It is also to smell and taste it – the tang of salt air in the coastal marshes, the fecund smell of wet vegetation in the Broads, the pungent aroma of wild garlic in ancient woodland in spring and, maybe less romantically, the occasional whiff of cattle slurry and freshly hosed farmyards. It is to experience wildlife too: the seeking out of Norfolk specialities and, more exciting still, chance encounters – sluggish grey seals on winter beaches on the North Norfolk coast, the deep boom of a bittern hidden in reedbeds, the spectacle of flocks of uncountable waders at the Wash, dragonflies and swallowtails in the Broads in summer; even the all-too-common experience of pheasants exploding from the undergrowth while crossing arable land. Perhaps more than anything, though, it is a sense of history, of change through time.

Any walk in Norfolk is a walk through history. Although the county might have become a backwater by the 19th century, in medieval times Norfolk was one of the most densely populated counties in England. Now it is among the least crowded. Unlike much of England, the Industrial Revolution never really took off in East Anglia as the region did not have the raw materials or power sources necessary for manufacture and so it was largely bypassed by the sudden and dramatic urban changes that took place throughout the North and Midlands. Norfolk's economic

revolution, if it could be called that, was earlier: between the 13th and 17th centuries when much of the land was given over to large flocks of sheep for the thriving international wool trade, and the county (or rather the county's landowners) grew wealthy on the profits. The wealth can still be seen today in lavishly decorated parish churches that seem to be disproportionately large for the small villages they service.

Despite its relative proximity to London, Norfolk still has a slightly isolated, 'end of the road' feel about it. Much of the county is, quite literally, at the end of the road as it does not lie on the route to anywhere else – if you have come to Norfolk, you have made a decision to come here and are not merely passing through. The fact that Norfolk is among the few counties in England that does not have a motorway going to it is something to be celebrated by those who prefer a quieter life. That is not to say that the county is backwards or insular as some might suggest, just that it has different priorities than simply getting somewhere as quickly as possible.

A BRIEF HISTORY

In 2010, the discovery of a haul of flint tools on a northeast Norfolk beach near Happisburgh pushed back the date of the first known human occupation of Britain by a quarter of a million years. The tools, which were estimated to be around 900,000 years old – the oldest

Gariannonum Roman Fort, Burgh Castle (Walk 11)

ever found in Britain – were probably those used by the hunter-gathering *Homo antecessor*, or 'pioneer man', who lived alongside mammoths and sabre-toothed cats in a Britain that was still attached to mainland Europe. At the time Britain's climate was becoming increasingly cool as it was entering an ice age and the population as a whole was probably no more than a few thousand at most. Much later, around 58,000BC, there is evidence of Neanderthal mammoth hunting sites in what is now Thetford Forest. The same Brecks region was also the scene for large-scale flint hand axe production at Grimes Graves in the Neolithic period around 5000 years ago. A millennium later, in the Early Bronze Age,

there appears to have been sufficient population to warrant the building of a ritual wooden structure – the so-called 'Seahenge' at Holme-next-the-Sea on the northwest coast near Old Hunstanton.

Evidence suggests that Norfolk has been continually farmed since the Iron Age, and hoards of coins and torcs found at Snettisham point to the presence of an organised and relatively sophisticated population back in the first century BC. The Iceni tribe were dominant in the region at the time of the Roman Conquest in AD43, and under the leadership of Queen Boudica they rebelled violently against Roman rule in AD60, creating widespread havoc in the region before being eventually subjugated. The Romans finally left in AD410 after building numerous roads and castles at Brancaster (*Branodunum*), Caister and Burgh Castle (*Gariannonum*) near Great Yarmouth. The next invaders were Anglo-Saxons who settled throughout Norfolk, which became part of the Kingdom of East Anglia ruled by an Anglo-Saxon dynasty. Vikings came a little later, attacking the county in the mid 9th century and killing King Edmund in Suffolk in AD869, leaving Norse names as testament to their presence in many settlements in the east of the county, particularly those that end in '–by' like Scratby, Filby and Hemsby.

Norwich, already an important Anglo-Saxon town, emerged as the region's most important hub under Norman rule and both its castle and cathedral were completed within half a century of the Norman Conquest of 1066. By the 14th century, Norfolk was the most densely populated region of England, partly due to intensive agriculture that cultivated the land and reared very large flocks of sheep as part of the burgeoning wool trade. Much of the county's remaining woodland was cleared for agriculture during this period. During the medieval period, the Church was central to everyday life in Norfolk and more churches, often financed by the wool trade, were built than in any other English county.

At the same time, monastic communities were established around the

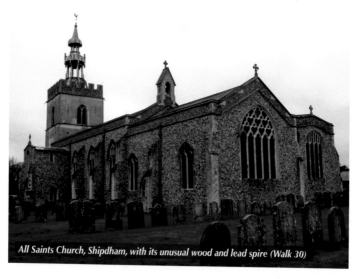

All Saints Church, Shipdham, with its unusual wood and lead spire (Walk 30)

county at Little Walsingham, Castle Acre, Thetford, Binham, Burnham Norton and North Creake. It was during this same period that the Norfolk Broads were inadvertently created by the extensive digging of peat for fuel in east Norfolk, the pits created eventually becoming filled with water to create a system of manmade lakes. During this same wool-boom period, Norwich, the county capital, enlarged to the extent that it soon became England's second city and would remain so until the early 18th century when it would be overtaken by Bristol. On the other side of the county from Norwich, King's Lynn developed to become an important port, and by the 17th century this was the busiest in Norfolk and a prominent member of the Hanseatic League, which promoted trade between England and northern Europe.

Compared to the rest of England, Norfolk was little affected by the English Civil War in the mid 17th century, although the county had been seriously shaken by Kett's Rebellion a century earlier in 1549, when 16,000 rebels under the leadership of yeoman famer Robert Kett temporarily occupied Norwich as protest against the forced enclosure of common land. Kett's men subsequently fought against the King's army, which with the aid of foreign mercenaries killed 3,000 of the rebels before capturing Kett and executing him for treason.

Many grand country houses were built in Norfolk in the 18th century,

including Holkham, Houghton and Felbrigg Halls. It was also around this time that the county became the cradle of the Agrarian Revolution, with landowners like Thomas William Coke ('Coke of Norfolk') and Charles Viscount Townshend ('Turnip Townshend') revolutionising farming with new modern methods and rotational systems. Having successfully made the transition from the production of wool and established itself as England's granary, Norfolk was seriously affected by a widespread depression in farming at the end of the 19th century as a consequence of the importation of grain from across the Atlantic. Many of the county's large estates became neglected or were forced to sell up and, in the aftermath of World War I, some were broken up into smaller units. World War II saw a population increase in the county, as many airfields, mostly bomber bases, were built in Norfolk because of its relative flatness and proximity to Germany. Although primary industries like farming and fishing have ceased to be big employers in the county since World War II, Norfolk still retains its essentially rural character into the 21st century.

LANDSCAPES

Although almost all of Norfolk lies below 100 metres in altitude there is considerable scenic variety within the county. Little of the land around the Broads rises more than a few metres above sea level, while some of the Fen region in the county's far west actually lies at sea level or below, the result of an ambitious drainage scheme that was begun by Dutch engineers in the 17th century and continued into the early 19th century, when wind-powered pumps were replaced by coal-powered steam engines.

The underlying geology is chalk but this only comes to the surface in parts of the west of the county. Most of what is seen on the surface is the result of fairly recent geomorphic activity – the land-shaping that took place at the end of the Ice Age when retreating glaciers laid down huge deposits of sand, mud and gravel on the underlying bedrock. In areas like the Brecks in the southwest of the county, the deposit was just a thin layer of sand, while elsewhere, large depositions of clay ensured that the resulting soil would be sufficiently fertile to provide for intensive farming for millennia. In North Norfolk, the Cromer Ridge, a low range of hills that marks the highest land in the county rising to 102 metres, was formed by old glacial moraines at the edge of the ice sheet during the last glacial period. The ridge, which lies just inland from the coast and extends west from Cromer, is characterised by large areas of open heath mixed with deciduous woodland.

The North Norfolk coast, most of which is designated an Area of

Eroding cliffs at Happisburgh with lighthouse and church in the distance (Walk 4)

Outstanding Natural Beauty (AONB), is characterised by sand and shingle beaches, salt marshes, freshwater lagoons, sand dunes, reedbeds and sand and shingle spits. While Blakeney Point is a classic textbook spit, Scolt Head Island to the west is an offshore barrier island that originated in much the same way. Both landforms are the result of east to west longshore drift. The whole of this coastline is threatened by climate change, with rising sea levels increasing the risk of coastal erosion and flooding. The threat of coastal erosion is even more acute further east in the stretch of coast that curves south between Cromer and Great Yarmouth, and large tracts of coastal land have been lost in recent years in coastal villages like Happisburgh.

East Norfolk is characterised by the Broads, a unique network of navigable lakes and waterways that consists of seven rivers and 63 broads, man-made lakes that were created by extensive peat-digging activity in the medieval period. The whole Broads area, although generally referred to as the 'Norfolk Broads', also partly belongs to a small area of north Suffolk. All seven of the rivers – the River Yare and its tributaries Bure, Thurne, Ant, Wensum, Chet and Waveney – are tidal to some extent, even as far inland as Norwich. Of the broads themselves, Hickling and Barton are the largest bodies of water,

Sailing towards Heigham Sound from the River Thurne (Walk 2)

Old Hunstanton's cliffs are composed of chalk and red sandstone layers (Walk 21)

while Breydon Water, the estuary of the River Yare near Great Yarmouth, also belongs to the Broads system.

The Brecks region of southwest Norfolk is a natural habitat shared with neighbouring Suffolk. One of the driest areas of England, the Brecks (or Breckland) are characterised by thin soils on top of chalk, which give rise to sandy heaths with unusual plant and animal species. As the soils here are light and easily worked, this was one of the first areas of East Anglia to be settled, deforested and farmed. A ready supply of flint for hand tools was another attraction for Neolithic settlers. Cleared for sheep farming and extensive rabbit warrens in the medieval period, the region was largely reforested in the early 20th century, with the creation of Thetford Forest in

1914. Large areas of the Brecks remain off-limits for walkers as they make up the Stanford Battle Zone Area, used for training by the British Army.

With the exception of the Fen country to the far west close to the Cambridgeshire and Lincolnshire borders, the west of Norfolk is generally more elevated than the rest of the county. Here, the chalk rises close to the surface in places, seen to good effect at Ringstead Downs and in the cliffs at nearby Old Hunstanton. The principal waterway in this part of the county is the River Great Ouse, which passes through Cambridgeshire before flowing through Downham Market into the Wash at King's Lynn. The River Little Ouse is an important tributary of the Great Ouse, which, along with the River Waveney to the east, delineates the border with Suffolk. Other important tributaries include the River Nar, which passes through Castle Acre and Narborough, and the River Wissey that joins the Great Ouse just south of Downham Market.

WILDLIFE

Norfolk is one of Britain's prime wildlife locations. Part of the reason for this is its geographical location in the east of England, with about half of its county boundary being coastal and jutting out into the North Sea. Other factors to consider are the county's low degree of urbanisation and relatively small population. The overriding factor explaining the county's diverse natural history, however, is its diversity of wildlife habitat. Few counties can claim to have such a diverse mix of coastal salt marsh, reedbeds, shingle banks, mud flats, sandy beaches, fens, dunes, ancient woodland, commons, acid heath, chalk downs, river estuaries, sand spits and river banks amongst its repertoire. None can claim these and the unique wetlands of the Broads and the sandy heaths of the Brecks as well.

The coastal wetland of the North Norfolk coast is celebrated for its rich birdlife, with the Norfolk Wildlife Trust (NWT) bird reserve at Cley-next-the-Sea being as close as it gets to 'birding Mecca', with its huge range of breeding birds, winter visitors, and passage migrants that often include rare vagrants. The whole of the coastal region is rich in wintering wildfowl, especially geese, breeding waders and rare reedbed birds like bittern and bearded tit. Mammals are plentiful too – grey and common seals, water voles and otters are all present – as are specialist maritime plants like shrubby sea blight, sea lavender and yellow-horned poppy.

In the Broads, typical species include grey heron, great crested grebe and marsh harrier, in addition to scarce species like common crane and Cetti's warbler among the breeding birds. Yellow water lily, common reed and alder are typical of the plants

Grey Heron reflected on the River Yare

here, while the rare swallowtail butterfly is locally plentiful, as is the Norfolk hawker and many other dragonflies.

The dry sandy heaths of the Brecks in the southwest of the county have a complex geology, with layers of sand overlying chalk. As a result, the vegetation found here consists of both chalk-loving and acid-dependent plants, and includes rarities like sand catchfly, spiked speedwell, military orchid and grape hyacinth. Breeding birds include woodlark and nightjar, as well as very rare stone curlew. A large area of the Brecks around Thetford has been afforested with conifers, which in turn provides valuable habitat for a number of species, especially on young or newly felled plantations. Deer – red, roe and muntjac – are plentiful in the area.

NATIONAL PARKS AND AONBS

Norfolk is home to the Broads, managed by the Broads Authority, which has equivalent status to a national park. The park, which at 303km² (117 square miles) also covers a small part of north Suffolk, was designated under the Broads Authority Act in 1988. Seven rivers and more than 60 broads and other shallow bodies of water make up the park that is contained within in the low-lying region that lies between Great Yarmouth, Norwich and North Walsham, and extends into Suffolk as far as Bungay on the River Waveney.

The Norfolk Coast Area of Outstanding Beauty (AONB), which at 451km² (174 square miles) covers much, but not quite all, of the Norfolk coast between King's Lynn and Great

Winterton Dunes Nature Reserve, just north of Winterton-on-Sea on Norfolk's northeast coast (Walk 1)

Yarmouth, was designated in 1968. The boundary, which extends up to 6km inland from the coast, was determined by the Countryside Commission (now the Countryside Agency). The Norfolk Coast Partnership was set up in 1991 to promote the sustainable use of the Norfolk Coast AONB. The main part of the AONB includes the coastal marshes, mud flats, dunes, shingle, reedbeds and grazing marshes of the North Norfolk Heritage Coast that stretches from Old Hunstanton to Weybourne. Other outlying parts of the AONB are found between Sea Palling and Winterton-on-Sea on the northeast coast, and north of King's Lynn along the Wash. The AONB contains world-famous bird reserves at Holme Dunes, Titchwell and Cley-next-the-Sea, and one of the country's finest dune systems at Winterton Dunes.

At a slightly lesser degree of national importance, there are also over 160 Sites of Special Scientific Interest (SSSI) in Norfolk, in addition to nearly 1300 County Wildlife Sites (CWS) and 27 Local Nature Reserves (LNR).

GETTING THERE AND BACK

Norwich, the Norfolk capital and the only city in the county, is well connected to London and the rest of the country. The frequent train service that runs between London Liverpool Street and Norwich takes less than two hours, while National Express coaches run between London Victoria and Norwich every two hours or so and

take just over three hours. Norwich is well connected by road for those with their own transport by means of the M11 motorway and the A11 dual carriageway from London and the south, which pass close to Harlow, Newmarket, Cambridge and Thetford en route to Norwich. Connections with the Midlands and the North are a little slower and road travel is by way of the A47 between King's Lynn and Norwich. A direct rail service operates between King's Lynn, Cambridge and London, and there are also direct services between Norwich and Sheffield, Manchester and Liverpool in the northwest. Most other train services to the Midlands and the North require a change of train in Peterborough or Ely. Norfolk's other principal town is Great Yarmouth, which is well connected to Norwich by both bus and rail services. For information on train times call National Rail Enquiries 'Train Tracker' service on 03457 484950 (calls cost no more than calls to geographic 01 or 02 numbers) or look on the internet – www.nationalrail. co.uk. For coach transport to Norfolk from London and elsewhere, contact National Express (0871 781 8181) or visit their website (www.national express.com).

Within Norfolk, there are frequent rail services between Norwich and Cromer and Sheringham on the Bittern Line (www.bitternline. com), which is integrated with the CoastHopper bus service between Cromer and Hunstanton. A Bittern

Walking on the Peddars Way near Harpley (Walk 32)

Line Ranger ticket gives you free travel on CoastHopper buses. The Wherry Lines (http://www.wherrylines.org.uk) rail service between Norwich and the east Norfolk coast follows two different routes, one to Great Yarmouth via Cantley and Berney Arms (a request stop) or Acle, and another to Lowestoft via Reedham and Haddiscoe. Another train route between Norwich and Cambridge stops at the Norfolk stations of Wymondham, Attleborough and Thetford along the way, while the Cambridge to King's Lynn service has a stop at Downham Market in the west Norfolk Fens.

Generally speaking, there are reasonable bus services throughout the county that are run by a number of different operators, although some more isolated villages may not have a weekend service and a few may only have a bus once or twice a week. Particularly useful bus services are the previously mentioned CoastHopper service run by Norfolk Green that extends all the way along Norfolk's north coast between Cromer and Hunstanton, and the First in Norfolk and Suffolk X1 express service between Great Yarmouth and King's Lynn that stops in Norwich, East Dereham and Swaffham along the way. A very useful facility for planning purposes is Traveline East Anglia (www.travelineeastanglia.co.uk; 0871 200 2233), which has links to timetables and route maps on its website.

For those travelling using their own car Norfolk roads are usually reasonably quiet, with the exception of the busy A47 and A11 trunk roads. The North Norfolk coast road can also be very busy in high summer, as can the routes that lead into the Broads. Car parking is generally adequate throughout the county, although the car parks in some coastal towns can sometimes be full in high season.

WHEN TO GO

There is no single 'best' season for any of these walks. Overall, probably the most pleasant months for walking are May, June and September, although April and October both have their merits in good weather. There is plenty to be said too for walking in autumn or even winter. Spring and summer bring flowers, insects, butterflies and lush vegetation (not always a bonus where stinging nettles are concerned) but autumn brings fungi and the beauty of turning leaves, and winter, flocks of overwintering migrants. For birdwatchers, the summer is actually the worst time for birds on the coast, and walkers may also find parts of some coastal routes busy with day-trippers en route to and from the beach. The Broads are also very busy in high summer, especially in the school holiday period when large numbers of visitors are drawn to the boat-hire centres of the area like Wroxham and Potter Heigham. The busiest months are July and August, especially on the coast, and services and amenities can become a little stretched at this time although this rarely presents much of a problem.

WHAT TO TAKE

Norfolk weather is usually reasonably mild, with little snow in winter. Clothing should be sensibly layered: Norfolk may be one of England's driest counties but it can still rain heavily when it chooses. The wind, too, can be fierce when it blows from the north and east, although this tends to be fairly infrequent. As with any route, walkers should check weather forecasts before setting out to determine whether wet-weather clothing is required for that day. Boots or substantial shoes and appropriate clothing should always be worn, and a small comfortable day-pack containing additional clothing, waterproofs, maps, food, drink and a camera should be carried.

In summer, insect repellent is a very good idea as mosquitoes can be a considerable annoyance in some woodland and marsh areas; midges may also be a nuisance on some stretches of the coast in still weather. Another irritation may be nettles along some routes, especially after a long period of cool wet weather – for obvious reasons, shorts are not always the best choice in such situations and long walking trousers might be considered a much better option. Sun cream will be necessary in summer, especially near the coast, where walkers may not be aware of becoming burned because of the cooling effect of a sea breeze. A sun hat is also advisable.

Shorts are fine in warm weather but there is always the potential hazard of brambles and nettles on overgrown paths, and so easily removable over-trousers (preferably with a zipped ankle gusset that goes over boots) are a good idea even if it does not look much like rain.

FOOD AND DRINK

Food and drink is usually available at pubs or tearooms close to the start and end points of the walks described in this book, and in some cases along the route as well. There are one or two exceptions where nothing is available along or close to the route and these are listed where applicable. Whatever the availability of food en route, it is always advisable to carry a supply of food and drink and 'emergency rations' in case of delay or exceptional circumstances. Places where refreshments are available are listed in the box at the start of each walk.

WAYMARKS AND ACCESS

For the most part, the public footpaths and bridleways that these walks follow are adequately signed. In many cases, the routes follow stretches of long distance trails for part of the way and as a rule these are well signed, with marker posts bearing the name and logo of that particular route – the acorn symbol for the Peddars Way and Norfolk Coast Path, the black wherry sail of the Wherryman's Way and so on. Occasionally signposts may be broken or half-hidden by overgrown foliage but the descriptive text and

map extract that accompanies each of these walks should be sufficient to ensure that the direction is clear.

SAFETY

Although the vast majority of the routes in this book involve the use of public footpaths, bridleways and farm tracks, there are occasional sections that require a limited amount of road walking. Short sections of these may be narrow country roads with no pavement: although these have been kept to a minimum, it is important to take due care along such stretches and be visible to drivers by means of bright outer layers that can be seen in poor light.

Walking in Norfolk is generally hazard-free. It is assumed that readers have basic navigational skills and are able to use a map and compass, and it goes without saying that walkers should follow the countryside code at all times and be particularly vigilant about shutting gates where there is livestock. Dog owners should keep their animals under supervision, especially when crossing farm land, and should note that dogs are not permitted in some nature reserves.

MAPS

Seven Ordnance Survey Landranger maps (1:50,000 scale) and ten Ordnance Survey Explorer (1:25,000 scale) cover the walks listed in this book. The four most useful OS

Landranger maps are 132, 133, 134 and 144.

OS Landranger

- 131 Boston & Spalding
- 132 North West Norfolk
- 133 North East Norfolk
- 134 Norwich & The Broads
- 143 Ely & Wisbech
- 144 Thetford & Diss
- 156 Saxmundham, Aldeburgh & Southwold

OS Explorer

- OL 40 The Broads
- 228 March & Ely
- 229 Thetford Forest in The Brecks
- 230 Diss & Harleston
- 236 King's Lynn, Downham Market & Swaffham
- 237 Norwich
- 238 Dereham & Aylsham

- 250 Norfolk Coast West
- 251 Norfolk Coast Central
- 252 Norfolk Coast East

USING THIS GUIDE

Given the largely flat terrain of Norfolk, all of the walks described in this book should be manageable by any reasonably fit walker. The forty walks vary in length between four and 12 miles, the majority lying somewhere midway between these extremes. The walks described follow footpaths and bridleways wherever possible, although there is also a limited amount of walking on farm tracks and quiet country lanes. No one part of the county has been favoured over any other and so, as well as coverage of highly popular and well-known areas like the North Norfolk coast,

Approaching Little Walsingham on the Greenway (Walk 25)

there are also walks that take in other equally distinct, if lesser known, parts of the county like the Brecks, the marshes of east Norfolk, the Yare and Waveney Valley, the Fens and the gently rolling farmland of the north Norfolk interior.

Each of the walks has been given an estimated time required for completion – this is merely an estimate based on walking at an average pace without stops. Stops for snacks, drinks, taking photographs or looking around churches and other historic monuments are not included in this estimate and time should be added on for these. Fast walkers may find the times given over-generous: they are merely intended as a guide and are not meant to be taken too literally.

As for transport to reach the start of the walk, no assumption has been made that the walker will have their own private means of transport. A few of the walks listed here are difficult to reach without a car but the majority are perfectly feasible using public transport, especially if based in Norwich or one of the larger towns like Great Yarmouth or King's Lynn. For those with their own cars, suitable places to park are suggested for each of the walks.

Each walk is accompanied by the appropriate section of the 1:50,000 OS Landranger map covered by the route, blown up to 1:40,000 (2.5cm to 1km) for greater clarity. In most cases, this, along with the written description, should be perfectly adequate for finding the way and completing the walk. There is, however, a lot to be said for having a copy of the appropriate OS map in order to see the wider picture – the area beyond the route itself. There is even more advantage in having the more detailed 1:25,000 OS Explorer map of the area, which will provide more information about the terrain and objects of historical interest along the way. For each walk, a precise start and end point has been given, along with six-figure grid reference, to avoid any confusion. Each walk also has the recommended 1:50,000 and 1:25,000 maps listed in the walk summary.

LONGER WALKS IN NORFOLK

All of the walks included in this book are circular, with little or no backtracking necessary. Some of the walks do, however, follow sections of long distance walks that go through the county. The best known of these are the Peddars Way, which begins in Suffolk but is mostly through west Norfolk, and the Norfolk Coast Path, which links with the Peddars Way at Holme-next-the-Sea and leads from here to Cromer (Cicerone publish a guidebook to these: *The Peddars Way and Norfolk Coast Path* by Phoebe Smith.) The main long distance routes that pass through Norfolk are listed in Appendix D.

1 NORTHEAST COAST AND THE BROADS

Canoeing at Horstead Mill near Coltishall (Walk 5)

WALK 1

Winterton-on-Sea

Start	Beach car park, Winterton-on-Sea (TG 498 198)
Distance	5 miles (8km)
Time	2hr
Map	OS Landranger 134 Norwich & The Broads, Outdoor Leisure 40 The Broads
Refreshments	Pub in Winterton, café at car park in summer
Public Transport	Public Transport Regular bus service from Great Yarmouth
Parking	Beach car park (closes at 4pm prompt in winter)

This coastal route beginning and ending in the village of Winterton-on-Sea takes in a variety of landscapes along the way. Most impressive of all is the large area of sand dunes immediately north of the village – a nature reserve with several rare and distinctive species. Elsewhere, the route follows farm tracks through woodland and quiet country roads with virtually no traffic.

Start at the beach car park, with fine views of the coast-line to the south across the dunes. Head towards the huts at the northern end of the car park then follow the track inland through the dunes towards the village and church. Reaching a group of houses, go past these to take the road to the right. At the end of a short row of houses a footpath continues across **Winterton Dunes** nature reserve. ▶ Walk through an area of scrub on the edge of the dunes. The main path runs in a northerly direction parallel to a fence, which, after a while, it runs right next to. Beyond the fence lies a large open area of heath with woodland beyond while to the right are high dunes separating the path from the beach.

A couple of notice boards at the entrance here give information about the wildlife that can be found in the dunes.

Winterton Dunes National Nature Reserve is unusual in that its dunes support acidic plant life: most dunes on the north Norfolk coast support calcareous flora. This factor means that the ecology here

WINTERTON-ON-SEA

Visiting Winterton-on-Sea back in 1722, the writer Daniel Defoe noted that many of the village houses were constructed from the timbers of wrecked ships. This part of the Norfolk coast has long been hazardous for ships because of its shifting sand banks and wrecking was a common pursuit in this region in the past. Today, thanks to its location at little more than sea level, the village is highly vulnerable to flooding and sea erosion, and a flood siren system has been installed.

If parking at Winterton beach car park in winter bear in mind that the gate is locked at 4pm.

is similar to that of dune systems along the Baltic coast. Natterjack toads breed here and the pools support both common and great crested newts as well as several species of dragonfly. In addition to numerous species of moth and butterfly, over 170 species of bird have been recorded here and wintering marsh harriers are frequently seen, as are nightjars in summer. Adders are common.

▸ The path veers away from the fence to pass through an area of birches before arriving close to **Winterton Ness**, where there is a crossroads of tracks. Turn left to walk through concrete defences that date from World War II and go through the gate to follow the track as it leads inland alongside the mixed woodland of **Winterton Holmes**. At the end of the woodland the track passes by wet grazing meadows. Continue past a track on the left to arrive at some isolated farm buildings and a concrete farmyard that may or may not be covered by a smelly layer of slurry. Follow the track around the field edge to the left next to a hedge. This soon turns sharply right to continue along a concrete farm track lined with willows before reaching another road at a T-junction. Turn left to

Alternative route: Follow the beach from the car park for about a mile and then head across the dunes to reach the fence. Follow this to the concrete defences.

Winterton Dunes Nature Reserve, a haven for birds and natterjack toads

follow Holmes Road, which has a large expanse of wet grazing meadows on either side of it, and turn left at the next junction.

Follow the road right at the corner by a cottage and continue past brick cottages to arrive at a junction with woodland ahead and a high brick wall to the left. Turn left along Low Road to pass **Burnley Hall** farm. Follow the road through a patch of woodland at **East Somerton** where the impressive **ruin** of St Mary's Church can be seen through trees to the right. This 15th-century Perpendicular-style ruin is covered in ivy and has an oak tree growing in its roofless chancel. The church once had its own parish and probably last saw use in the late 17th century.

Continue in the same direction past a barn conversion and pond. Turn right at the white house, then left towards Winterton's lighthouse and church tower immediately ahead. Where the road swings around to the right take the track that continues in the same direction as the church. Continue along this until passing Low Farm then take the footpath to the right that leads past allotments to Holy Trinity and All Saints Church.

> **Holy Trinity and All Saints Church**, like many churches along the Norfolk coast, has a tall Perpendicular tower that stands as a beacon to those out to sea. However, despite local rumour that it is 'a herring and a half higher', the tower is actually 35 feet shorter than that of Cromer's St Peter and St Paul Church.

Turn left at the road to pass a green with the village sign and, a little further on, the Fisherman's Return pub. Go past the post office and The Loke on the right to follow the road to the beach and the car park.

WALK 2

Start	Medieval bridge, Potter Heigham (TG 420 185)
Distance	5½ miles (8.8km)
Time	2hr 15min
Map	OS Landranger 134 Norwich & The Broads, Outdoor Leisure 40 The Broads
Refreshments	Pub and cafés in Potter Heigham
Public Transport	Regular bus service from Great Yarmouth and North Walsham
Parking	Plentiful parking at Lathams store just north of bridge (three-hour limit)

Beginning and ending at Potter Heigham, a Broadland village heavily involved in the summer boat hire trade, this is a surprisingly tranquil walk once away from the village. The route skirts the southern side of Hickling Broad, a large expanse of fresh water that is home to rare wildlife unique to the Broads, before following a stretch of the River Thurne, one of northeast Norfolk's principal waterways.

Note that this walk passes through part of Hickling Broad National Nature Reserve and the Norfolk Wildlife Trust that manages it has a no dogs policy on the reserve.

Start at the north side of the medieval bridge and walk along the road away from the river past boat hire offices on the left and Lathams store on the right. Go past a caravan park on the left before coming to the junction of Station Road on the right. Turn right to reach the main A149 then cross this carefully to walk along Station Road where it continues on the other side. At the T-junction turn right along Church Road and continue past bungalows and thatched cottages to reach St Nicholas Church, a pretty thatched building with a round tower and a 14th-century octagonal belfry above. Inside is a splendid hammerbeam roof, wall paintings and a rare 15th-century brick font.

ROUND TOWER CHURCHES

Norfolk has 124 existing round tower churches, far more than any other county (Suffolk has 38, Essex has six) in England. Although they are found largely in East Anglia, there are also church towers of similar design in Germany. Most round tower churches are of Saxon origin but the reason for their construction is still open to debate. It is probable that they were built because of a lack of suitable building materials for square towers (corners are hard to build using flint), or even that they may have originally been defensive structures (unlikely).

Bird-rich reedbeds at the edge of Hickling Broad

Carry on past the junction with the church on your right and at the corner take the footpath that leading right then left along a track by a hedge that heads north towards woodland ahead. At the edge of the wooded area you will come to a sign marking the entrance to Hickling Broad nature reserve. Continue through the wet woodland area and go over a footbridge to reach a path close to the reedbeds at the edge of the broad. Turn right to follow the path along the southern edge of **Hickling Broad**.

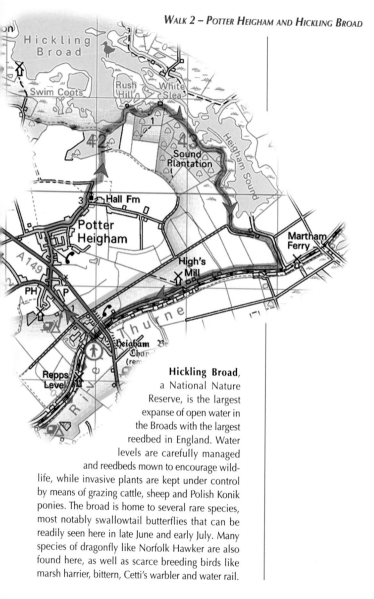

Hickling Broad, a National Nature Reserve, is the largest expanse of open water in the Broads with the largest reedbed in England. Water levels are carefully managed and reedbeds mown to encourage wildlife, while invasive plants are kept under control by means of grazing cattle, sheep and Polish Konik ponies. The broad is home to several rare species, most notably swallowtail butterflies that can be readily seen here in late June and early July. Many species of dragonfly like Norfolk Hawker are also found here, as well as scarce breeding birds like marsh harrier, bittern, Cetti's warbler and water rail.

Some parts of the route described may be overgrown in summer, especially the section between Heigham Sound and the River Thurne.

After passing a bird hide at **Rush Hill** scrape, the path veers right alongside a dyke and the woodland of **Sound Plantation** before crossing more open grazing beside **Heigham Sound**. Eventually, a dead straight farm track leads off left over a bridge and across fields (a slightly shorter, alternative route back to the village). Keep going to reach the narrow channel that links Hickling Broad with the River Thurne system. ◀

Pass a small thatched building next to the water and continue alongside the channel to reach the main river ahead. Follow the footpath along the bank of the River Thurne to the right, which after a while joins a concrete path as it begins to pass a line of riverside chalets. The path diverts inland a little at a pumping station and then continues along a wider gravel track before diverting again around a small inlet at High's Mill, a converted windmill. From here the path leads past a continual line of chalets before eventually passing underneath the A149 road bridge. Potter Heigham's medieval bridge is reached almost immediately after.

Potter Heigham's medieval bridge, a hazard for navigation

Potter Heigham's **medieval bridge**, which is thought to date from 1385, is considered to be the most difficult to navigate in the entire Broads system. Many hire-boat novices have come unstuck here as only small cruisers can pass beneath it at low tide, usually with the assistance of a pilot.

WALK 3
North Walsham

Start	North Walsham Market Cross (TG 282 303)
Distance	8 miles (12.8km)
Time	3hr
Map	OS Landranger 133 North East Norfolk, Explorer 252 Norfolk Coast East
Refreshments	Pubs and cafés in North Walsham
Public Transport	Regular bus and train services to Norwich and Cromer
Parking	North Street Car Park

This varied walk on the edge of the Broads, which begins and ends in the historic market town of North Walsham, takes in rolling countryside, picturesque hamlets and a disused railway and canal along the way. The walk also follows the Weavers' Way long distance path for some of its route.

Begin at the Market Cross in the town centre. Following the direction indicated by the Weavers' Way signpost, walk slightly uphill towards the Yarmouth Road. ▶ Go past St Nicholas Church with its partially ruined tower and the North Walsham town sign. At the junction, turn right past supermarkets and cross a roundabout to continue along Grammar School Road. Pass the police station and an entrance to a park before turning left down Filby Road.

At the end of the bungalows follow the Weavers' Way signpost along the path that leads between two fields. Climbing gently, there are good views east towards

Weavers' Way is a 62-mile (99km) long distance footpath linking Cromer, Aylsham, North Walsham, the Broads and Great Yarmouth. Its name reflects the once important weaving industry in the area.

35

MARKET CROSS

North Walsham's original Market Cross dates from 1550 but this, along with much of the town, was destroyed by a great fire in 1600. The cross was rebuilt in 1602 and fitted with a chiming clock in 1899. The building was restored several times during the 20th century and lost its weathervane to an enemy bomb during World War II. Its current lead roof and restored clock date from 1984 and the cross is now both a National Monument and a Grade I listed building.

The route of the old North Walsham and Dilham Canal

the coast. Turn left along a minor road that has a belt of trees to its right. Reaching the Happisburgh road, turn right passing White Horse House, formerly a pub, on the left then turn right along Holgate Road opposite the telephone box. This descends downhill past **White Horse Common**. Turn left at the next junction, then right to **Meeting House Hill**. Go past the Meeting House, with graves in the front garden, then turn right.

Follow the signpost to turn left along the edge of a field. Continue to reach a minor road with an

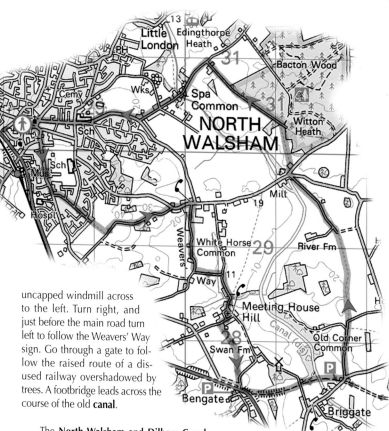

uncapped windmill across to the left. Turn right, and just before the main road turn left to follow the Weavers' Way sign. Go through a gate to follow the raised route of a disused railway overshadowed by trees. A footbridge leads across the course of the old **canal**.

The **North Walsham and Dilham Canal**, which ran between the River Ant at Smallburgh and Swafield, was the only canal ever constructed in Norfolk. Designed for the relatively wide girth of Norfolk wherries, its construction involved the canalization of the upper reaches of the River Ant. Its main purpose was to carry animal carcasses to the bone mills at Antingham although the wherries also carried flour, grain and even coal. The canal fell into decline in the late 19th century and is currently only navigable for two miles between Smallburgh and Honing Lock.

Arriving at the long former platform of Honing station, go through to the car park and bear left at Station Cottage along Corner Common Road to climb gently. Just after a road to the left that leads to Corner Common Farm go through the gap in the hedge at the next corner to continue straight on along a track across fields. This eventually meets with a farm track. Turn left towards the houses ahead. The track passes a couple of bungalows and houses to emerge at a meeting of three roads, to the left of which is an interesting old **mill** complex. At the junction, turn left towards the mill then, just before the bridge, right along a farm track alongside a stream and mill pond towards a gate. At the next gate turn right to follow the permissive path that leads right towards woodland ahead.

Reaching the wood at **Witton Heath**, go through the gate and turn left to follow the track, a sunken lane with high banks on either side, along the edge of coniferous woodland. Passing **Bacton Wood** Farm, turn left at the road and go over a small bridge with old mill buildings to your right. At Manor Road, turn right and continue with Spa Common on your right. Walk past an infants' school to continue across the crossroads to head towards the distinctive tower of St Nicholas Church and, just beyond it, the starting point at Market Cross.

WALK 4

Happisburgh

Start	Happisburgh beach car park (TG 385 308)
Distance	4½ miles (7.2km)
Time	1hr 50min
Map	OS Landranger 133 North East Norfolk, Explorer 252 Norfolk Coast East
Refreshments	Pub in Happisburgh
Public Transport	Bus service from North Walsham and Stalham
Parking	Happisburgh beach car park

Happisburgh, pronounced 'Haysboro', is well known locally for its distinctive red and white lighthouse. The village is also infamous for the savage sea erosion that has already claimed much of its land and buildings and is continuing to make the village crumble into the sea despite expensive protective measures being taken. There is nowhere better in Norfolk to see the relentless march of nature as sea destructively and unapologetically reclaims land.

This is a particularly invigorating walk in winter, when the sea is at its wildest.

From the car park walk towards the ramp that leads to the beach before turning right to walk along the path that follows the cliff path east. Follow the path, taking care to keep away from the cliff edge itself. ▶ After about half a mile, approaching a group of wooden houses close to the cliff edge, the path goes through a broken fence. Turn right here to follow the path diagonally across a field to pass a couple of isolated buildings in the middle of it. This path soon turns into a farm track: follow this and where another track crosses it turn right in the direction of the lighthouse.

The track swings around to the left below the lighthouse to join Lighthouse Lane. Turn right and follow the lane past houses and the entrance to the lighthouse to

There are excellent views here east along the coast and west back to Happisburgh lighthouse and St Mary's Church.

HAPPISBURGH LIGHTHOUSE

The oldest working lighthouse in East Anglia, dating from 1790, Happisburgh Lighthouse is also the country's only independently operated lighthouse. At 26 metres tall, and with distinctive red and white bands, this has long been a landmark in the flatlands of north-east Norfolk. The lighthouse has a number of open days between March and September when visits are possible – details are available at www.happisburgh.org/lighthouse/open-days.

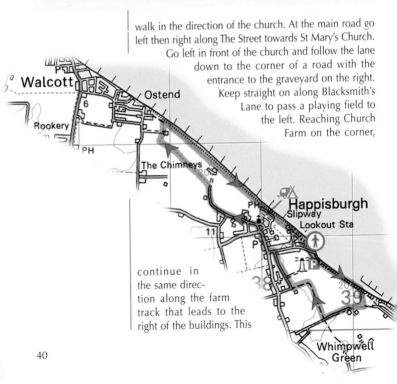

walk in the direction of the church. At the main road go left then right along The Street towards St Mary's Church. Go left in front of the church and follow the lane down to the corner of a road with the entrance to the graveyard on the right. Keep straight on along Blacksmith's Lane to pass a playing field to the left. Reaching Church Farm on the corner, continue in the same direction along the farm track that leads to the right of the buildings. This

Fast eroding Happisburgh cliffs

continues past another set of farm buildings and, just after this, where there is a gate and a sign prohibiting unauthorised vehicles, turn left to follow the field boundary northwest.

Continue, following the raised bank between fields, until just before reaching the bungalows of **Walcott** ahead. Just before the track swings left, a footpath sign – which might be obscured by vegetation – indicates the way across the field to the right towards another post. Follow this to join a green track that leads to the cliff edge at **Ostend**, from where the dwellings of Bacton and the industrial complex of the Gas Distribution Station are visible to the northwest. Turn right to follow the cliff path east past the Happisburgh Coast Watch hut back towards Happisburgh village. Follow the track through the caravan park beneath the church. ▸

Note Erosion is so rapid near Happisburgh Caravan Park that the track may well be diverted in the near future.

At the far end of the caravan park continue walking in the same direction until reaching a former road that erosion has caused to disappear abruptly over the cliff edge. Turn right towards the lighthouse then go left at the road to return to the car park and starting point.

WALK 5

Horstead and River Bure

Start	Recruiting Sergeant pub, Horstead (TG 264 196)
Distance	4½ miles (7.2km)
Time	2hr
Map	OS Landranger 133 North East Norfolk or 134 Norwich & The Broads, Outdoor Leisure 40 The Broads
Refreshments	Pubs and cafés in Horstead and Coltishall
Public Transport	Regular bus service to Norwich and North Walsham
Parking	Rectory Road near church

This short, scenic circuit takes in an attractive stretch of the Bure just before the river starts to wind its way through the Broads system at Wroxham.

Note: The footpath that follows the east bank of the River Bure may be very overgrown with reed and nettles in high summer.

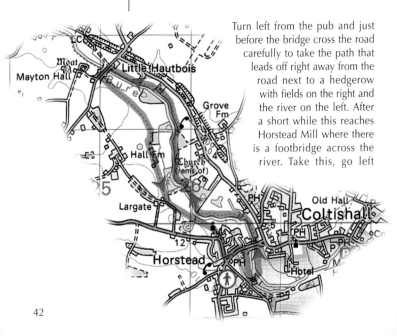

Turn left from the pub and just before the bridge cross the road carefully to take the path that leads off right away from the road next to a hedgerow with fields on the right and the river on the left. After a short while this reaches Horstead Mill where there is a footbridge across the river. Take this, go left across a picnic area then right across a footbridge over the sluice to continue left along the path alongside a line of beech trees. Go over a couple of small footbridges to reach the road where a small village green effectively serves as a traffic island with a garage in the middle of it. This is the village of **Coltishall**, which has pubs, a few shops, a couple of food takeaways and a tearoom.

> **Coltishall**, a Saxon settlement mentioned in the Domesday Book, was once the centre of an important malting industry. Wherries used to load and unload here en route to Yarmouth or Aylsham.

Turn left towards the bridge, cross the road and go through a gate to take the footpath that leads off to the right immediately before the bridge. The path leads along the east bank of the River Bure, at first passing the rear of Coltishall gardens and small landing stages with boats. Cross a footbridge, where another watercourse joins the

A shady stretch of the River Bure north of Horstead

river at Hautbois House, and continue as the path meanders beneath willows in a more or less westerly direction. Horstead's All Saints Church can be seen to the left across the river.

> **Little Hautbois** and **Hautbois House**, both pronounced 'Hobbis' in Norfolk, take their name from the de Haut Bois family who acquired land in the area following the Norman Conquest. Hautbois Hall was built in the Tudor period, probably on the site of an existing manor house. Such was the extravagance of its construction that the descendents of the original builder are thought to have gone bankrupt as a result.

Historic Mayton Bridge over the River Bure at Little Hautbois

As the path gently veers north the farm buildings of Church Farm become visible up the hill to the right. The path eventually comes right down to the water's edge and continues beneath trees until reaching an area of

open pasture next to the water. Continue as far as the bridge then go through a kissing gate to reach the road. The grand Tudor buildings of **Mayton Hall** can be seen ahead on the south bank of the river. Turn left to go over historic Mayton Bridge, which spans the former course of the river.

> **Mayton Bridge** at Little Hautbois is a red brick double-span bridge with four-centred arches that dates from the early 16th century. Once spanning the former course of the River Bure, the bridge has splayed parapets at either end as well as recessed shelters with brick seats. The bridge is designated both a Grade II listed building and Scheduled Ancient Monument.

Turn left along the farm track that lies directly opposite the entrance to Mayton Hall Farm to head south-east back towards Horstead. Follow the track that has a hedgerow to the left and large fields rising up to the right. Soon a distinctive Italianate water tower belonging to **Hall Farm** comes into view across the fields to the west. Go over a stile and, coming to a wood, turn right to follow it round the corner to reach another stile. Continue south across meadows and alongside a fence towards an isolated farmhouse ahead.

Go over stile into a little lane at **Largate** and turn left. Leave the lane at the corner to follow the path across a meadow and enter a belt of shady woodland to cross a footbridge over a stream and reach another meadow where the tower of **Horstead**'s All Saints Church rises ahead behind trees. The path leads into the churchyard and then into Church Close. Turn left down Rectory Road to walk back to the main road to return to the starting point at the Recruiting Sergeant.

2 SOUTH NORFOLK, THE YARE AND WAVENEY

Two churches side by side at Shotesham – one ruined, one still functioning (Walk 12)

WALK 6
River Chet and Hardley Marshes

Start	White Horse Inn, Chedgrave (TG 361 992)
Distance	8 miles (12.8km)
Time	3hr 15min
Map	OS Landranger 134 Norwich & The Broads, Outdoor Leisure 40 The Broads
Refreshments	Pubs and cafés in Chedgrave and Loddon
Public Transport	Regular bus service to Norwich and Beccles
Parking	Car park at Chedgrave staithe and at All Saints Church

The River Chet flows eastwards between the villages of Loddon and Chedgrave before joining the larger River Yare. This walk combines a pleasant riverbank walk with a short section through Hardley Marshes before returning along quiet farm tracks and country lanes to its starting point in Chedgrave, an attractive Yare Valley village.

Starting at the White Horse pub, walk north along the main street to a crossroads and turn right by some shops. Go past the church and continue along a quiet country lane past Chedgrave Common on the right before passing beneath power lines. Soon the water of **Hardley Flood** becomes visible away to the right. At the next junction, go right along the bridleway that has a Wherryman's Way sign. Follow this broad grassy track along the edge of fields and then woodland on the right as it climbs gently up Broom Hill. At the crossroads of tracks, from where nearby Hardley Hall can be seen to the right, continue straight on to reach the **River Chet**.

Hardley Flood is an area of shallow lagoons and reedbeds that serves as a spillway fort the River Chet. The flood was created by flooding farmland in the 1940s and is now a Site of Special Scientific Interest (SSSI), part-managed by the Norfolk

Hardley Cross on the River Yare, marking the point where Norwich's jurisdiction of the river ends and Great Yarmouth's begins

Wildlife Trust, with a nationally important breeding population of pochard, gadwall and shoveler ducks.

Turn left to follow the path along the raised bank of the river towards its confluence with the **River Yare**. Approaching the larger river, the imposing features of the sugar factory at Cantley to the north on the other side of the River Yare come into view, as do the houses of Nogdam End just across the Chet to the east.

The path joins the River Yare at **Hardley Cross**, a restored historic cross, after passing a pond to the right.

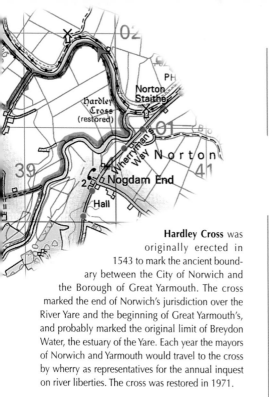

Hardley Cross was originally erected in 1543 to mark the ancient boundary between the City of Norwich and the Borough of Great Yarmouth. The cross marked the end of Norwich's jurisdiction over the River Yare and the beginning of Great Yarmouth's, and probably marked the original limit of Breydon Water, the estuary of the Yare. Each year the mayors of Norwich and Yarmouth would travel to the cross by wherry as representatives for the annual inquest on river liberties. The cross was restored in 1971.

Follow the path left along the River Yare to veer right and left past a windmill on the opposite bank before reaching a staithe. Turn left along the footpath next to the staithe and go past the moorings to reach the end where there is an information board. Turn right here to follow a signed footpath along the edge of a field. This soon joins a green lane next to a pair of cottages. Continue to reach a thatched cottage, then bear left along **Hardley Street** to pass more cottages and farm buildings. Reaching a junction with a large oak tree, continue to the right along Church Lane. Pass farm buildings to arrive at another junction and turn right following the Langley sign.

Go along **Langley Street**, through the village and past a couple of farms and a converted chapel. After Great

Yard Farm take the next left along Gentleman's Walk. This very quiet lane climbs gently uphill to give good views back over the river and marshes before reaching a row of houses before a corner. Follow the lane round the corner to head downhill beneath power lines once more to arrive at a crossroads. Head straight on along Snow's Lane into Chedgrave. Reaching a T-junction, turn left then immediately bear right to arrive at the village crossroads by the shops. Continue a short distance to return to the White Horse Inn.

WALK 7

Outney Common and Earsham

Start	Bungay Castle, Suffolk (TM 335 898)
Distance	5½ miles (8.8km)
Time	2hr 15min
Map	OS Landranger 134 Norwich & The Broads, 156 Saxmundham, Aldeburgh & Southwold, Outdoor Leisure 40 The Broads
Refreshments	Pubs, cafés and restaurants in Bungay
Public Transport	Regular bus service to Norwich, Lowestoft and Diss
Parking	Priory Lane car park, Bungay

This walk is centred on Bungay, which is actually just in Suffolk. Most of this walk, however, follows a picturesque loop of the River Waveney around Outney Common that lies within the county of Norfolk. The Waveney Valley, which marks the boundary of both counties, is something of a place apart that has characteristics of both Norfolk and Suffolk as well as an individual character that is entirely its own.

Start from the Castle on a mound just west of Bungay's market place. Take the steps that lead down to Castle Lane, turn right then right again on Earsham Street and then almost immediately left onto Outney Road. Follow

Footpath through woodland at Outney Common

Outney Road to the end then take the footpath to the right that leads to a footbridge across the **A143**. Once across the busy road, turn right towards the Golf Club along the track parallel to the road. Walk along this parallel to the busy road to skirt a small lake near a roundabout. The track turns left around the water to join a gravel track.

Turn left at the Outney Common Trails sign and then right through a gate to follow a grassy path. Go through another gate to continue straight ahead across **Outney Common** to reach a footbridge across a river channel. Follow a farm track and go through a gate to continue across the meadow to reach a footbridge across the River Waveney into Norfolk. Cross another footbridge over another channel then turn left through a gate and into a meadow soon after to follow the Angles Way west.

Go diagonally across the meadow up towards a gate between two oak trees. This climbs a sharp rise alongside gnarled Scots pines to reach a ridge from where there is a good view to the south over the Waveney Valley, albeit obscured by trees to some extent. Follow the ridge above **Ditchingham Lodge**, with the steep tree-filled slope to the left and fields to the right. The track broadens out

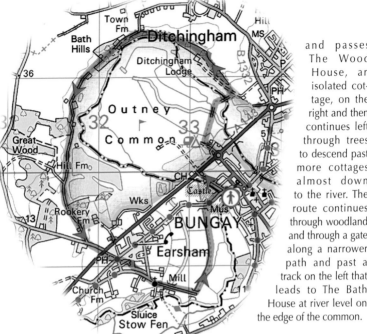

and passes The Wood House, an isolated cottage, on the right and then continues left through trees to descend past more cottages almost down to the river. The route continues through woodland and through a gate along a narrower path and past a track on the left that leads to The Bath House at river level on the edge of the common.

The nearby village of **Ditchingham** has several literary connections. Sir Henry Rider Haggard (1856–1925), author of *She* and *King Solomon's Mines*, lived and worked for many years at Ditchingham House and is buried in the village's St Mary's Church. Henry's daughter, Lilias Rider Haggard (1893–1968), also buried in the churchyard, wrote a trilogy of books about Norfolk life and lived for many years at The Bath House on Outney Common. The Norfolk-based German writer W G Sebald (1944–2001) describes his visit to Ditchingham churchyard at the end of his most famous book *The Rings of Saturn*.

The way continues along a farm track and then joins a road at Valley Farm before passing a large gravel works on the left with warning signs about lorries turning. Walk along the road past a large lake on the left and **Hill Farm** up on the right. Turn left at the next road and, on reaching the A143 ahead, cross the road to head straight ahead and follow the Angles Way sign into Earsham.

At Station Road take the footpath just left of the war memorial to cross a road and follow a wrought iron fence to reach another road. Turn left to pass All Saints Church on the right and continue to the end of the track ignoring the signs indicating both Bigod Way and Angles Way to the right. Go over the footbridge and continue to the end of the farm track past fields of cattle before crossing another footbridge and turning left over a stile to follow the footpath along the bank of a tributary next to a stream.

The two towers of **Bungay Castle** can be seen across the field to the right before reaching the Earsham to Bungay road at a bridge. Go through a gate up to the road and turn right. Go over the bridge past the Bungay sign and turn right into Castle Lane to return to the walk's starting point.

Cattle grazing on Outney Common by the River Waveney

Bungay Castle, today little more than a ruin with two crumbling towers, was once an impressive fortress set in a naturally defensive location on a mound in the centre of Bungay. The fortress was constructed in the 12th century by Hugh Bigod, Earl of Norfolk, whose family had inherited land in the area following the Norman Conquest. However, Bigod's rather vainglorious attempt to take Norwich from King Stephen II precipitated his downfall and he was forced to surrender the castle to the king, who ordered it to be destroyed. Demolition was delayed on payment of a large fine, and the castle survived to be reinforced more than a century later by Hugh's descendent Roger, who created the twin-tower gateway that is still seen today.

WALK 8

Rockland St Mary and Claxton

Start	Rockland Broad staithe (TG 328 047)
Distance	6½ miles (10.4km)
Time	2hr 45min
Map	OS Landranger 134 Norwich & The Broads, Outdoor Leisure 40 The Broads
Refreshments	Pub in Rockland St Mary and at Beauchamp Arms on river
Public Transport	Regular daytime bus service to Norwich
Parking	Rockland Broad staithe car park

This walk follows the Wherryman's Way for some of the way, taking in one of the less well known broads, an attractive stretch of the River Yare, minor country lanes and the pleasant rolling countryside of the Yare Valley east of Norwich.

As with any walk along paths close to water, stinging nettles can be a problem in summer, especially following wet weather. In these circumstances the wearing of shorts is ill-advised.

Rockland Broad

Begin at the staithe, opposite the New Inn pub at Rockland St Mary. ▶ Walk along the footpath beside the moored boats that is signed as part of the Wherryman's Way and follow the path that skirts the edge of **Rockland Broad** to the right hand side. To the right are open fields of rough grazing; to the left the broad can be distinguished through the willows and alders that surround it. At the northern of the broad the path continues along a channel to reach the River Yare. Turn right and follow the riverbank east towards the Cantley sugar beet factory in the distance ahead on the other bank.

A staithe is a landing stage for boats, often an inlet cut away from a river: the word derives from Old Norse.

The **Wherryman's Way** is a 35 mile-long recreational route that runs from Norwich to the coast at Great Yarmouth largely along the banks of the River Yare – the south bank as far as Hardley Cross, then the north bank between Reedham and Great Yarmouth. The route takes its name from the flat-bottomed sailing barges, known locally as a wherries, that used to ply the River Yare and the navigable waterways of the Broads. The walking route is well-marked with many information boards, audio points and commissioned pieces of sculpture along the way.

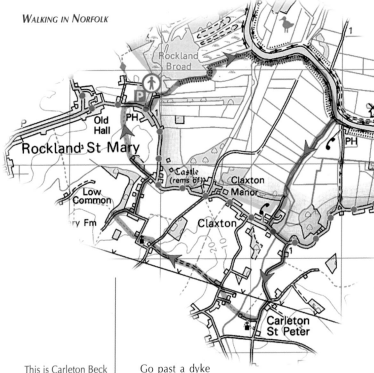

This is Carleton Beck Outfall, which in summer is usually covered in yellow water lilies.

Go past a dyke and Claxton Pumping Station to reach a gate and then, just before reaching the Beauchamp Arms **pub** on the river ahead, turn right to walk along the dyke. ◄

Arriving at a gate, continue along the farm track towards the road. Turn left at the road and walk along the verge. Go over the bridge that crosses a stream then take the next junction to the right towards **Carleton St Peter**. Follow this quiet road past thatched cottages and a footpath to the left to continue to a junction by a farm. Turn right along Ferry Road and follow this until reaching a track off to the right just before a church. Take the path that skirts a house and continues over a footbridge over a stream and bends to the right around paddocks before coming out at a track. Turn left, then right at the road before taking the next track to the left by pylons and a large square Georgian building that was formerly a Baptist meeting house.

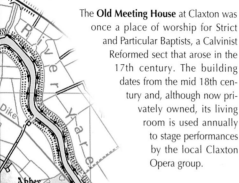

The **Old Meeting House** at Claxton was once a place of worship for Strict and Particular Baptists, a Calvinist Reformed sect that arose in the 17th century. The building dates from the mid 18th century and, although now privately owned, its living room is used annually to stage performances by the local Claxton Opera group.

Follow the track uphill past open fields to reach a crossroads of tracks from where there are good views north across the fields to the Yare Valley.

Approaching Claxton church and village

Walk downhill towards **Claxton**'s thatched Church of St Andrew. At the road, turn right then immediately left to follow a footpath to the right of the church.

Cross the road and take the footpath that runs along the left hand side of the house opposite. Follow this along a field boundary to reach a track by a plantation of trees. Turn right along the track and then left at the corner by farm buildings. Walk past cottages and stables and go over a stream, and at the corner just before reaching a main road take the track that leads sharp left. At the end where it turns right towards a house take the lower track that skirts a garden on the right before following the footpath along a field boundary next to a hedge on the left. This bends round to the right at the next field boundary to join a track alongside a field boundary as new houses on the road ahead come into sight. Turn right at the road to return to the staithe and New Inn.

WALK 9
Surlingham

Start	Surlingham St Mary's Church (TG 305 065)
Distance	4½ miles (7.2km)
Time	1hr 45min
Map	OS Landranger 134 Norwich & The Broads, Outdoor Leisure 40 The Broads
Refreshments	Pubs by the river in Surlingham and at Coldham Hall
Public Transport	Regular daytime bus service between Norwich and School Lane, Surlingham
Parking	St Mary's Church

Although Surlingham lies close to Norwich, the village has a peaceful rural feel to it. This short walk follows the Wherryman's Way for a short distance along the River Yare before cutting through a meander of the river by means of tracks and quiet roads to return to the river at a riverside pub. From here the route passes through marshy woodland and crosses to return to the starting point via a ruined church close to the village's existing one.

Starting at the car parking area in front of St Mary's Church gate, walk to the corner of the churchyard wall. ▶ Take the path opposite that leads north downhill beside a cottage towards the river. This soon comes to a sluice, where you enter the Church Marsh RSPB reserve before arriving at the river. Turn right to follow the track that leads along the south bank of the River Yare. In summer, the river here may be busy with holiday cruisers; in winter, it is usually very quiet. Follow the riverside path that is flanked with hawthorn and sloe bushes to reach an observation shelter that overlooks the marshes to the south. A little way past this a path to the right leads to a bird hide.

Take note of the large stone that was probably used as a horse mounting stone in the past.

Surlingham has two wildlife reserves, the **Church Marsh RSPB reserve** and the **Ted Ellis reserve** at Wheatfen Broad. The Church Marsh reserve has marsh harriers, kingfishers, water rail and reed and sedge warblers in summer, and in winter sometimes attracts gadwall and shovelers and occasionally bittern. Wheatfen Broad was set up by local naturalist Ted Ellis on a 130-acre site of woodland, fen and marshland.

Sailing craft on the River Yare near Surlingham Ferry

On arrival at a footpath off to the right that leads to Church Marsh, continue straight on along the permissive path beside the river. Go through a gate and across the green by the Surlingham Ferry **pub** then turn right up the road that leads away from the river. This passes through wet alder woodland before reaching a junction. Turn left and follow the road out of the village. Continue along the road past a junction where the road bends around to the right and take the bridleway to the left, signed 'Wherryman's Way', which leads along a track past houses and gardens. This soon bends to the right before joining a metalled road. Turn left and continue to reach Coldham Hall **pub** and restaurant. Walk through the pub garden to the green next to the river – Brundall's **Marinas** lie immediately opposite across the river. Turn right through the gate to reach the sailing club then turn right along the footpath by the staithe that leads west, parallel to the road you have just come along, to reach Coldham Hall.

Follow the path through marshes to join a track by a house. Turn right and continue to reach the main road.

Ruin of St Saviour's Church, Surlingham

Bear right at the road back towards Surlingham and walk past houses and a road to the right that leads to Coldham Hall before taking a footpath off to the left through a gate alongside a hedge. Pass allotments on the right and continue on the footpath between fields to reach the corner of a road. Continue along the road in the same direction before turning right at the next junction along Ferry Road. Go past cottages to the right then look out for a footpath to the left at a bend in the road. Take the footpath that leads along a hedgerow to reach a gate.

Turn left along another footpath, which leads past a shooting range and goes through a gate to lead beneath the ruins of St Saviour's Church, where a small plaque marks the burial place of local naturalist Ted Ellis and his wife Phyllis.

Ted Ellis (1909–1986) was keeper of natural history at Norwich Castle Museum from 1928–56 and a prolific natural history writer and broadcaster in his later years. For forty years he lived with his family at a remote cottage at Wheatfen Broad, Surlingham amongst 130 acres of woodland and fen. This later became the Ted Ellis Nature Reserve, a recognised SSSI and one of the last tidal marshes of the Yare Valley. The Wheatfen reserve, consisting largely of fen, sallow carr and reedbeds, is now managed by the Ted Ellis Trust.

After a short detour to the ruins of the old church follow the track that leads gently uphill past a sluice back to St Mary's Church car park and the starting point.

WALK 10

Burgh St Peter and 'The Triangle'

Start	Burgh St Peter village hall (TM 468 935)
Distance	6 miles (9.6km)
Time	2hr 15 min
Map	OS Landranger 134 Norwich & The Broads, Outdoor Leisure 40 The Broads
Refreshments	Pub in Wheatacre and pub at Waveney River Centre (seasonal Easter to October)
Public Transport	Five buses a day to and from Beccles
Parking	Burgh St Peter village hall car park

This peaceful circuit explores one of Norfolk's most isolated corners: the triangle of land enclosed by the, now defunct, Beccles to Great Yarmouth railway on one side and a sharp bend of the River Waveney on the other two. With excellent views over the river and Waveney marshes, this walk also offers the bonus interest of a very unusual church along the way.

Turn right out of the village hall car park and then left down Wash Lane. At the corner, where the road bends right, take the footpath that leads across fields next to a hedge. The track climbs gently to pass a wide track to the left. Ignore this to continue in the same direction to

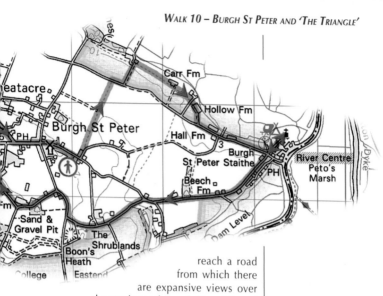

reach a road
from which there
are expansive views over
the marshes to the north. Turn right and
then left down a track towards farm buildings. Just before
the farmhouse take the footpath to the right that leads
across fields parallel to the edge of the marshes below.

'The Triangle' is a local name that was sometimes
used to refer to the parishes of Aldeby, Wheatacre
and Burgh St Peter in southeast Norfolk. Bound on

*A muddy farm track
in 'The Triangle'*

two sides by a bend of the River Waveney and on the other by the now-dismantled Beccles to Great Yarmouth railway, the triangle of land so defined has something of the feel of an island to it. There is no through road here, just a quiet single-track lane that links the farmsteads on the marshland edge. To the north, east and south a large flat area of marshes lies between the relatively high land of 'The Triangle' and the river itself.

Continue straight on across the next field to cross the driveway to **Carr Farm** just before its entrance. Follow the path to cross another track and go through a gate to walk through a meadow towards the cottages of **Hollow Farm** ahead. Go through another gate before taking the permissive footpath to the right that soon joins up with a track on the other side of the cottages. Turn right to follow this back to the road then turn left. ◄ Walk past farm cottages and a road to the right to climb to arrive at a corner with the Waveney Inn opposite and Church Lane off to the left. Turn left to walk past **Waveney River Centre** up to the church.

The road is narrow here with no verge, although traffic should not be a problem on this quiet lane.

Brick ziggurat tower of St Mary the Virgin Church, Burgh St Peter

Burgh St Peter's **Church of St Mary the Virgin** is one of Norfolk's oddest churches, as its tower is in the form of a five-section ziggurat (or, as some have fancied, a collapsible square telescope). The body of the church dates from the 13th century but the tower is an 18th-century addition, supposedly inspired by the Italian travels of William Boycott, the rector's son.

A dynasty of Boycotts served the church for a continuous period of 135 years and Charles Cunningham Boycott, the son of the second Boycott rector, gave the term 'boycott' to the English language when he behaved badly over absentee rents in Ireland and was socially ostracised as a result.

Returning to the corner from the church, go left to follow the road uphill towards **Beech Farm**. ▶ Walk past a woodland copse and a former rectory on the right to pass a road that joins from the left. Take the next road to the left, signed 'The Marshes', and follow this steeply downhill before climbing up towards the farm complex of **The Shrublands**. Go past **Boon's Heath**, where there is a large (modern) stone with runes set in the hedgerow, one of seven marking the boundary of Aldeby parish that were erected as a millennium project. Go right at the next junction along Mill Road and then left down Taylor's Road. At **Oaklands Farm**, at the bottom, turn right to pass cottages and go over a crossroads before arriving at a T-junction. Turn left down Rectory Road past a row of cottages before taking the footpath to the right that leads along a fence and a hedgerow to enter a small wood just before arriving at a road.

Turn right past **Wheatacre**'s All Saints' Church with its unusual brick and flint chequerboard tower, then right at the junction to pass the White Lion pub before reaching the Beccles road. Turn left past the village sign and the old board school building before continuing over the crossroads to reach the converted Methodist chapel that serves as **Burgh St Peter**'s village hall.

To the left are tremendous views across the Waveney marshes into Suffolk and Lowestoft in the distance.

WALK 11
Burgh Castle

Start	Queens Head pub, Burgh Castle (TG 481 052)
Distance	4½ miles (7.2km)
Time	2hr
Map	OS Landranger 134 Norwich & The Broads, Outdoor Leisure 40 The Broads
Refreshments	Pubs in Burgh Castle and Belton, and at Burgh Castle Marina
Public Transport	Regular bus service from Great Yarmouth
Parking	English Heritage car park, Burgh Castle

Burgh Castle is one of Norfolk's most evocative Roman sites, with a striking location at the confluence of the Yare and Waveney rivers. This short figure-of-eight walk, as well as taking in the Roman fort and the village's charming church, follows a bracing stretch of the Angles Way long distance footpath along the bank of the River Waveney south of the confluence. This is a classic Broadland landscape of long views, vast reedbeds, marshes, wading birds and windmills.

Starting with the pub behind you, turn right and walk past the junction and a row of council houses to arrive in front of St Peter and St Paul Church, a round towered church in a quiet, leafy spot separated from the rest of the village. Just beyond the entrance to the churchyard, a gate leads to a footpath signed 'Circular Walk'. Take this and descend through trees to soon arrive at marshes next to the southern end of Breydon Water.

Although the shooting of wildfowl used to be very popular in the estuary, **Breydon Water** is now a RSPB nature reserve and the UK's largest protected wetland. Large numbers of wading birds like golden plover and dunlin overwinter here, while species such as shelduck and oystercatcher breed here in summer. The western end of the estuary marks the confluence of two of Norfolk's largest rivers, the

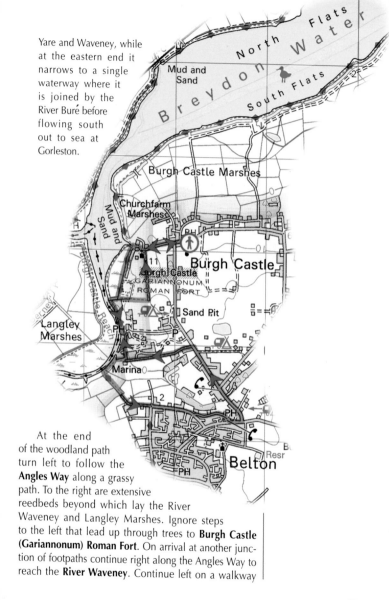

Yare and Waveney, while at the eastern end it narrows to a single waterway where it is joined by the River Buré before flowing south out to sea at Gorleston.

At the end of the woodland path turn left to follow the **Angles Way** along a grassy path. To the right are extensive reedbeds beyond which lay the River Waveney and Langley Marshes. Ignore steps to the left that lead up through trees to **Burgh Castle (Gariannonum) Roman Fort**. On arrival at another junction of footpaths continue right along the Angles Way to reach the **River Waveney**. Continue left on a walkway

Remains of Roman Fort at confluence of Yare and Waveney rivers, Burgh Castle

over a dyke and continue along a narrow path with fences on both sides towards the **marina** ahead. Reaching the Fisherman's Inn, take the path that goes around the pub and past a small cottage before turning right past a road barrier to walk along the lane behind the marina. At the far end of the marina, turn right at a junction next to cottages to continue along the Angles Way back towards the river. Arriving at the river path, walk for a short distance past moorings before turning left inland along a track by a pumping station.

The **Angles Way** is a 93-mile (149km) long distance path that runs along the Waveney and Little Ouse rivers between Great Yarmouth and Thetford in the Norfolk Brecks.

Burgh Castle (Gariannonum) Roman Fort was one of a string of forts built by Romans in the late third century AD to protect what was then known as the 'Saxon Shore' – the vulnerable eastern coastline of England between the Solent and the Wash. This fort, known as *Gariannonum*, was responsible for controlling the entrance to the River Waveney. Saxons later occupied it, and a motte-and-bailey castle was built within the walls following the Norman Conquest. The site was also possibly the location of *Cnobheresburg*, the seventh-century monastery founded by Saint Fursa, the first Irish missionary in southern England. Although the walls are still sturdy and, in places, well-preserved, much of the original flint and tile of the walls has been lost in the centuries since the fort's demise, plundered for local building work.

Follow this path through a gate to reach houses at the edge of **Belton**. Leave the Angles Way here to continue along the road in the same easterly direction as before. Bear left down St John's Road to pass woodland on the left, and reaching the road junction and a pub, turn left, and then left again at a roundabout, to follow Butt Lane north. Go past the junction of the Bradwell road to the right and just after Bure Valley Holiday Park turn left along Porter's Loke, a private road with pedestrian access. This follows a green lane to arrive back at the junction of the Angles Way next to the marina. Turn right here to retrace your steps past the marina, pub and narrow footpath path between fences once more. Having turned inland at the walkway, leave the Angles Way at the next junction, continuing in the same direction uphill alongside the south wall of **Burgh Castle (Gariannonum) Roman Fort**.

After diverting left to explore the Roman fort, continue in the same direction to reach a track by a hedge and turn left to follow it to pass St Peter and St Paul Church on the left. Turn right at the road junction to return to the Queens Head and the walk's starting point.

WALK 12
Shotesham

Start	Shotesham All Saints Church (TM 246 990)
Distance	7½ miles (12km)
Time	3hr
Map	OS Landranger 134 Norwich & The Broads, Explorer 237 Norwich
Refreshments	Pub in Shotesham
Public Transport	Limited daytime bus service from Norwich and Harleston
Parking	Shotesham, All Saints Church

Ruined churches and the rolling South Norfolk countryside make this a pleasant and historically interesting walk. This walk is probably at its best in early summer when orchids and other scarce wild flowers may be seen in the meadows.

Wildflower meadow at Great Wood near Shotesham

From the church walk down the slope to the road then follow the Boudica's Way sign that leads through woodland beneath the church. The path follows a small stream and climbs up slightly to emerge at the edge of the wood before crossing an open field. Continue through a gap in the hedge, climbing very slightly, until you meet a farm track and turn left. This skirts the northern end of Great Wood to pass through wild meadows filled with orchids in early summer. Turn left at the bottom of the field to reach isolated houses at **Stubb's Green**, where **Boudica's Way** continues along a track to the right following a hedgerow towards **Little Wood**.

Boudica's Way (or Boudicca Way) is a 36-mile long distance footpath between Norwich and Diss in south Norfolk. Named after the legendary Iceni queen, whose tribes lived here under Roman occupation, the route passes by the former Venta Icenorum at Caister St Edmund close to Norwich

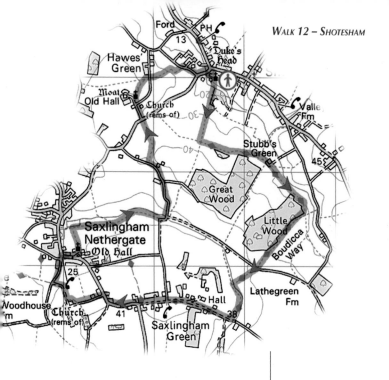

and ends in the Waveney Valley next to the border with Suffolk.

Reaching the wood, go through a stile and continue along its eastern perimeter until reaching another stile at the corner of the wood. Turn right to follow the path along the edge of the wood south until you meet a path that leads diagonally left across an arable field. Take this to soon arrive at a minor road.

Cross the road to take the footpath across the field. Turn left at another path next to a ditch. Follow the hedgerow towards a white house ahead to reach the road at **Saxlingham Green**. Turn right along the road and continue past cottages and a disused telephone box opposite a junction. Carry on to a Give Way sign at

Ruined church in a wood near Saxlingham Nethergate

the corner of the main Hempnall–Saxlingham road and continue past Low Farm and around a corner before taking the bridleway along Plummer's Lane that leads off left. This skirts a small wood that has the ruins of an old **church** just inside it.

The bridleway continues along a sunken green lane to reach a junction. Turn right here (Boudica's Way continues straight on) to follow another deep holloway that leads to a crossroads next to the war memorial at **Saxlingham Nethergate**.

Holloways are roads or lanes that over time have fallen lower than the land that surrounds them. This is the result of erosion, water and traffic wearing them down over the years. They are often associated with ancient foot and cart routes and processional ways to churches.

Turn right past the rectory and take the path left to St Mary's Church. Walk through the graveyard and follow the footpath that leads north past a small wooded area. Meeting another footpath, turn right and, crossing another footpath, follow this across the fields for about half a mile before arriving at the corner of a minor road. Turn left and follow this past Greatwood Farm to turn right through a gap in the hedge along a footpath just after a small house on the right. This follows the right of a field before reaching pylons where it bends to the left to cross a field directly towards the towers of two churches, one of which is ruined. At the road go straight up past the ruins of St Martin's Church before taking the footpath that leads to the right of its replacement, St Mary's. ▶

This path follows a hedgerow to reach a track. Turn right along this to reach a minor road then continue across, following the footpath towards Shotesham's All Saints Church. Turn right at the road to go downhill to the junction, then left to return to the church and the walk's starting point.

St Martin's Church, now just a picturesque ruin, is one of four churches that used to stand in Shotesham parish.

WALK 13
Fritton Common

Start	Fritton Common (TM 225 927)
Distance	4 miles (6.4km)
Time	1hr 30min
Map	OS Landranger 134 Norwich & The Broads, Explorer 237 Norwich
Refreshments	Pubs in Hempnall and Long Stratton
Public Transport	Bus service from Norwich to Long Stratton (2½ miles away)
Parking	Fritton Common lay-by by telephone box

This short walk starts and ends at one of south Norfolk's largest village commons and follows a combination of quiet minor roads and public footpaths through mixed farmland.

Note: there may be bulls in some of the fields in the early stages of this walk.

Start out at the telephone box at the northwest of **Fritton Common**. Walk north to the top of the common, go round

A blunt warning!

the top on the road then take the track that leads off to the left. This passes a barn conversion and old stables to veer east away from the common. Reaching a white house, another track leads off to the left. Follow this to cross a field towards a gap in the hedge ahead. Continue in the same direction along a green lane to arrive at a gate into a field. Turn right to head south along a track across fields to arrive at a lane.

Fritton Common is typical of many of the commons that used to be found in south Norfolk villages, few of which survive today. Its short grass, rich with plants like orchids and cowslips, is maintained traditionally by means of light grazing by cattle, and its 12 ponds contain a variety of wildlife that include rare water beetles and great crested newts. The 70-acre common is a designated SSSI.

A shady green track near Fritton

WALK 13 – FRITTON COMMON

Turn left
along Steppings Lane, which bends gently to the right
as it climbs slightly. Arriving at a sharp left-hand corner,
take the track that leads off to the right. This follows a
shady green lane that is almost engulfed by hawthorns
on either side. The path emerges at the edge of a field
and threads around a small brook before continuing
along the edge of fields in the same southwest direction. Go through a gate and turn right over a concrete
bridge towards another gate then walk around the edge
of another field to the left and continue towards a house
to reach the road at **Shelton Green**.

Turn right and follow the road as far as Lodge Farm.
Take the footpath to the left into the trees. Follow the
path to go over a stile into a field and turn right. Head
diagonally across the field towards a belt of trees, then,
emerging from the trees, continue in the same direction
along a hedgerow towards the **school** buildings on the
road ahead. Cross a footbridge over a stream, continue
across the fields towards the school and go over a stile
to join the road. Cross the road and go to the right of the
school along a footpath alongside a hedge. Shortly after
passing a footpath off to the left, a path to the right leads

off towards a plantation to the north. Take this to reach the road, turn left and then right to walk along the west side of Fritton Common to return to the starting point.

WALK 14
Harleston and Redenhall

Start	Harleston Market Place (TM 245 833)
Distance	6½ miles (10.4km)
Time	2hr 30min
Map	OS Landranger 156 Saxmundham, Aldeburgh & Southwold, Explorer 230 Diss & Harleston
Refreshments	Pubs and cafés in Harleston
Public Transport	Regular bus service to Norwich, Diss and Bungay
Parking	Market Place (limited) or Bullocks Fair Close, just off The Thoroughfare

Starting and ending in the pretty market town of Harleston, on the Norfolk side of the River Waveney, this walk explores the gently rolling Waveney Valley east of the town and visits the village of Redenhall, home to the parish church of St Mary that is shared by Harleston.

Harleston's clock tower and Magpie Inn sign

With the Magpie Inn behind you, walk north along The Thoroughfare with the clock tower to your right. Go past the Post Office and Union Street on the right and Bullocks Fair Close on the

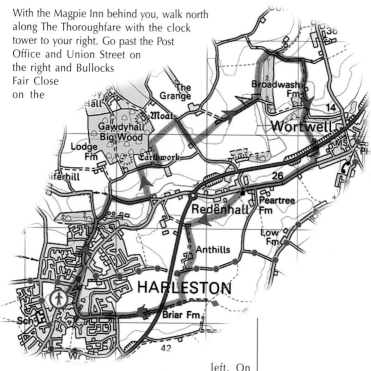

left. On meeting Broad Street, which joins from the right, continue a little further before turning left up along Station Road. Continue along Station Hill and past the old railway station yard, now a builder's merchants. Head downhill past bungalows, then go over a bridge before turning right, uphill, along a narrow lane, with the tower of Redenhall church soon coming into view across fields to the right.

Harleston is a small town in south Norfolk, close to the Suffolk border, which developed around the trading that began here in 1259 when the settlement was granted the right to hold a market and

Quiet country crossroads just outside Harleston

fair. The minaret-like clock tower on the Market Place used to belong to St John's Chapel of Ease but the rest of the building has long disappeared.

The Magpie Inn, opposite the clock tower on the other side of the Market Place, is an old coaching inn – Churchill and Eisenhower are reputed to have met here during World War II. Unusually, the town has no medieval parish church of its own but shares St Mary's Church at Redenhall, as the village belongs to the same single parish of Redenhall with Harleston.

Reaching a crossroads, with just a track to the left, turn right in the direction of the church and, just before reaching a bridge and a group of houses, turn left along the footpath that follows a line of oaks uphill along a field edge towards a wood. At the lane in front of **Gawdyhall Big Wood** turn right, then turn left along the footpath that runs along a field edge parallel to a driveway to a house on the edge of the wood. The path skirts the house to the right before leading diagonally across the field in a north-east direction towards the farm buildings of **The Grange** ahead, just across the valley. Follow this to reach the road at a road junction, turn right and continue as far as a pair of cottages to the right, then take the footpath to the left uphill along a field edge. ▶

Arriving at a group of farm buildings, continue with the hedge on your left to follow a farm track in the same direction. Continue downhill with oaks on either side of the track to pass an area of woodland on the left. Reaching a copse of trees ahead, turn left to follow the footpath sign where the main track veers to the right. Go over a stile into pasture and follow the field edge alongside coniferous woodland before going over another stile on the opposite side of the field. Carry on over two more stiles and a footbridge over a stream before reaching another stile and footbridge just before the bend of a minor road.

Turn right along the road to walk uphill for about a quarter of a mile before taking the farm track off to the right that leads gently downhill past a converted barn. Go through a gate to continue along a narrow track through woodland to pass **Broadwash Farm** on the right. Walk across a footbridge then take the footpath to the right that skirts a field before climbing up a steep rise to reach a stile. Follow the path across the field, keeping just to the right of the converted farm building complex to reach the A143.

Carefully cross the busy road and continue straight across along the public footpath before turning right along the bottom of gardens and then left to reach the road at the western end of **Wortwell** village. Turn right to follow the footpath alongside the road into **Redenhall**. Arriving at St Mary's Church, go through the gate into the churchyard and walk around to the front of the church before continuing along the narrow footpath that leads west from the church alongside a dyke and fence. Follow the path that continues along a track between fields towards farm buildings ahead. Just before reaching the A143, the track turns sharply left to head towards the buildings and trees of **Anthills** ahead.

The track skirts Anthills on the left hand side before veering right to reach a minor road. Turn right, then

The path across the field from Gawdyhall Big Wood may be very muddy in wet weather.

almost immediately left, on another footpath along a field edge and hedgerow. This soon reaches a track that crosses left to right – the route of the Angles Way. Turn right to follow this past a pond to reach the A143. Cross the road, then go over a stile to continue along the farm track past the buildings of **Briar Farm**. Where the farm track joins a road, turn right to pass through new housing development on the edge of town. This road eventually swings right to reach older housing before arriving at a junction just after a chapel on the left. Turn left to walk past the white Corn Exchange building just before arriving back at the market place in **Harleston**.

WALK 15

Cringleford and River Yare

Start	Car park near Cringleford Bridge on Newmarket Road (TG 021 061)
Distance	4½ miles (7.2km)
Time	2hr
Map	OS Landranger 134 Norwich & The Broads, Explorer 237 Norwich
Refreshments	Café in Earlham Park, pub in Eaton
Public Transport	Regular bus service to and from Norwich city centre
Parking	Small car park just off road to the left, northeast of Cringleford Bridge, almost opposite supermarket entrance

This walk along the River Yare and around University Broad at Norwich's southwest edge is surprisingly peaceful, with many opportunities for viewing wildlife, especially birds. In addition to a tranquil stretch of river there is also the opportunity to see the Norman Foster-designed Sainsbury Centre for Visual Arts in the leafy grounds of the University of East Anglia.

From the car park, take the path west that runs parallel to the Newmarket Road above. This soon reaches Cringleford's medieval bridge and a large mill pond with

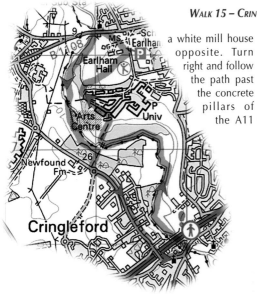

a white mill house opposite. Turn right and follow the path past the concrete pillars of the A11 overhead. ▶ Turn left over the footbridge to continue along the riverside path that follows the River Yare on its east bank, with marshes and rough grazing to the right and woodland across the river to the left – herons and king-fishers are commonly seen along here. The river meanders north past reedbeds, full of singing sedge warblers in summer, before veering sharply to the left after widening out.

Take the small footbridge across the brook to go left through a section of woodland and follow the footpath, now a walkway, to emerge at a footpath that skirts the south side of UEA Broad.

UEA Broad is entirely man-made, an artificial lake created when wet marshland was dug out for gravel extraction in the expansion of the university from 1973 to 1978. The 'broad' has softened and natural-ised with time to become a haven for breeding birds like great crested grebes, plants such as water-lilies, and plentiful dragonflies. It is also popular with local fishermen.

Despite constant traffic noise from the nearby A11, otters are sometimes seen on the river near Cringleford Bridge, especially in the early morning.

Turn left and follow the edge of the broad, with the ziggurat-shaped concrete buildings of the **University of East Anglia** to the right over the water. Reaching a large footbridge at the end of the broad – the 'Mathematical Bridge', a copy of the bridge over the River Cam at Queens' College, Cambridge – and turn right to walk around the western end of the broad following the edge of woodland towards the **Sainsbury Centre for Visual Arts** ahead. At the end of the woodland to the left, with the arts centre straight ahead on the rise, turn left away from the broad to follow a track through the edge of the wood. This path plunges deeper into the wood, turning right to head north before coming out at a road next to a roundabout and university buildings.

The **Sainsbury Centre for Visual Arts** was opened in 1978, designed by Norman Foster as his first major public building. It houses the extensive modern art collection of Sir Robert and Lady Sainsbury that contains works by artists such as Alberto Giacometti, Francis Bacon and John Davies as well as a collection of open air sculpture that includes bronzes by Henry Moore.

A wooden walkway beside the River Yare at Cringleford near Norwich

Continue through the trees across the road, bearing right at a junction of paths, to reach Earlham Park, an open area of mature parkland with scattered trees. Walk uphill towards the white café hut along a track lined with oak trees. Go past a track to the left that leads to the café hut and dovecote beyond to continue uphill towards **Earlham Hall**, which soon becomes visible through the trees.

Turn left between two oak trees to reach a pathway then turn right. Take the diagonal path to the left past ornamental conifers to reach a formal box planting. Go through the gate in the wall to walk past the rear of Earlham Hall along a tarmac road. Just before reaching another surfaced road, take the path to the left through trees to meet a track that goes left to the café and right to an ornamental brick dovecote. Bear right to walk to the dovecote.

From the dovecote, descend to the river bank and go left along it until reaching a surfaced road by a bridge. Turn right, then left, to follow the west bank of the river as far as the Mathematical Bridge encountered earlier. Turn right at the bridge to follow a broad track uphill through woodland. Turn left at the road at the top and go past bollards and a parking area to walk along Colney Lane into

Cringleford's medieval bridge on the outskirts of Norwich

83

Cringleford Bridge was built as a replacement for an earlier wooden one that was swept away in a flood in 1519.

Cringleford. This continues through a leafy residential area before crossing over the A11 dual carriageway after about 20 minutes walking. Turn left at the corner by a large house with a Dutch gable, at one time the village pub, and follow Newmarket Road over Cringleford Bridge back to the starting point at the car park. ◄

WALK 16
New and Old Buckenham

Start	St Martin Church, New Buckenham (TL 088 906)
Distance	4½ miles (7.2km)
Time	2hr
Map	OS Landranger 144 Thetford & Diss, Explorer 237 Norwich
Refreshments	Pub in New Buckenham
Public Transport	Regular bus service to Norwich
Parking	On street near church, or at New Buckenham village hall

This walks links two Buckenhams, Old and New, and follows the Tas Valley Way long distance footpath for part of the way. Of interest along the route is New Buckenham Castle, which has the ruins of a circular keep within an inner bailey surrounded by a water-filled moat. Also of note on this walk is nearby New Buckenham Common, a large expanse of ancient grazing land, two medieval churches and some lovely South Norfolk countryside.

New Buckenham is really not that new – the village developed around the castle built by the Norman baron William d'Albini, whose family had been given the manor of Buckenham by William the Conqueror. New Buckenham was actually a planned market town with an orthogonal medieval grid system, although there are few medieval buildings that survive today. New Buckenham Common, at 37 hectares, is one of the largest in the county, and has been grazed by sheep and cattle for at least

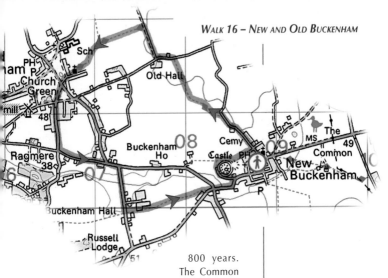

800 years.
The Common
– which is an SSSI with over 150 species of flowering plants, including a large population of green-winged orchids – became a nature reserve in 1984, when it was sold to the Norfolk Wildlife Trust.

Facing the church, turn left to walk north up Cuffer Lane past Moat Lane and a **cemetery** on the right. Go past allotments and farm buildings as the road swings left then, at the next corner where the road veers right, take the footpath off to the left to go through a gate where a signpost indicates the Tas Valley Way.

The **Tas Valley Way** is a 25-mile (40km) long distance path between Norwich and Attleborough that roughly follows the course of the River Tas through south Norfolk.

Cross over a stile and follow the footpath between fields. Pass a copse of trees and go through a gap in the hedgerow to continue through another field. The footpath emerges at Harlingwood Lane, a quiet minor road. Turn left past a modern house to the right then turn right along the track opposite **Old Hall**.

*New Buckenham
village green seen
from beneath Market
Cross*

After about 300m, before reaching the field barn ahead, go left across the field to follow the footpath west. After about the same distance again this joins with another footpath coming from the north: turn left to follow this to reach a paddock that is skirted by permissive path alongside the hedgerow. With the playing fields of Old Buckenham High School to the right, go along a fenced track between paddocks towards the church. Enter the churchyard through the gate.

Leave the churchyard by the gate on the south side, turning right along the lane. Turn left at the playground and go straight across the main road past the **Old Buckenham** war memorial on the left and a large area of common land the right. Follow the residential road that leads south from the crossroads to reach the hamlet of **Ragmere**, then turn left to join the B1107, which joins from the left. Follow this for a short distance before turning right down Doe Lane, a minor road. Meeting public footpaths leading right and left, go left through a gate to follow a grassy track alongside a hedge. This follows the edge of fields over stiles towards a line of houses ahead.

At the end of the houses the path meets the road just before a junction. Turn left, cross over the B1077 and continue along the B1117 towards New Buckenham, walking its footpath for a short way before taking the road that leads off sharply to the left at St Mary's Chapel. Follow this track left around the moat and mound of the castle, passing the gatehouse (usually locked) at its south-west side and continue around until meeting a track coming from the left. Go right to skirt the northern side of the castle mound and follow the track alongside a hedgerow to come out on the road by the village hall. Turn right to return to the church. ▸

St Mary's Chapel, New Buckenham, a converted 13th-century chapel that is now a private dwelling, once also served as a barn.

New Buckenham Castle was built in the reign of King Stephen (1092–1154), grandson of William the Conqueror, two miles to the southeast of an earlier castle at Old Buckenham that was demolished to provide materials for the founding of an Augustinian priory. At New Buckenham, the foundations of a circular stone keep, approximately 60 feet in diameter and one the earliest and largest examples in England, survive, although the four-storey castle was largely demolished in 1649, leaving just earth ramparts and a large moat.

Tower of St Martin's Church, New Buckenham

87

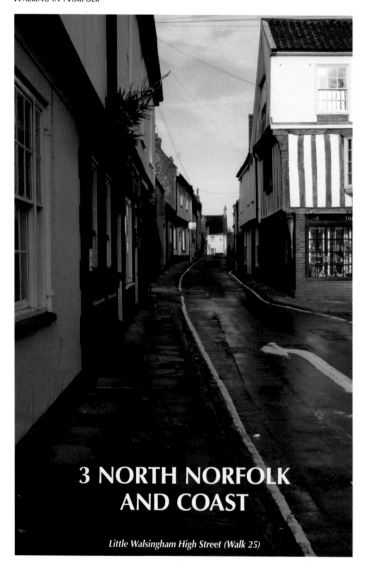

3 NORTH NORFOLK
AND COAST

Little Walsingham High Street (Walk 25)

WALK 17
Sheringham and Beeston Regis

Start	Sheringham seafront (TG 158 436)
Distance	5 miles (8km)
Time	2hr
Map	OS Landranger 133 North East Norfolk, Explorer 252 Norfolk Coast East
Refreshments	Pubs and cafés in Sheringham
Public Transport	Regular bus and train service to Cromer and Norwich
Parking	Car park next to Sheringham railway station

This varied walk starts and ends at the seaside resort of Sheringham, once an important crab and lobster fishing centre. The route climbs up away from the coast to one of Norfolk's highest points on Beeston Regis Heath, and traverses part of the high (for Norfolk) ridge that is the scenic backdrop to this part of the coast. This may be 'flat' Norfolk, but on this walk you will find some of the steepest hills in the county.

With the sea behind you at the seafront, walk a little way back inland along the high street and take the first left along Wyndham Street. Continue along Beeston Road, past pebble-built cottages and Priory Road to the left before taking the next left, a service road that leads along a footpath to another road that passes beneath a railway bridge. Go under the railway bridge then immediately turn left along a track that leads diagonally away from the road across a grassy area, the edge of Beeston Regis Common. Carry on diagonally across the common following paths that lead south towards the main road ahead.

At one time **Sheringham** consisted of two separate communities: Upper Sheringham, where life was mostly centred on farming, and Lower Sheringham, which had a mixture of farming and fishing. The arrival of the railway in the 19th century allowed the

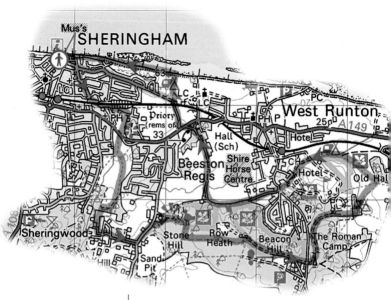

town's crabs and lobsters to be transported easily to the lucrative London market. At one time there were over 200 boats engaged in fishing of one kind or another; these days there are fewer than ten.

Carefully cross the busy A149 just to the right of a large lay-by and follow the footpath across the common that leads diagonally away from the road. This soon reaches an information board by a pond with some benches. Continue along the main track with the pond on your right to go along a short boardwalk through trees. The path then passes through an open area of gorse until it reaches a wooded area close to a hedge with bungalows on the other side. Keep going, ignoring a path that veers off right, to climb gradually until the path turns sharply to the right at the edge of the wooded area.

The path continues right through oaks and birch past a fingerpost indicating another track off to the right across an open area. Shortly after this, take the footpath to the left that leads between two fences passing a large isolated house to the left. Reaching **Sheringwood**, turn left at the

corner by a bungalow, following the road right at the next corner then left again to reach a junction. Turn left past a post box in a fence and continue, passing two roads that join from the left, to follow the road, first around to the right then sharp left. Follow this, climbing quite steeply, up to the road ahead.

Turn left at the road, heading gently downhill past a large quarry off to the right as the North Sea and Sheringham come into sight once again across the fields to the left. Follow the road carefully (no pavement) around a couple of corners before taking the public bridleway that leads up to the right alongside a fence. This leads up through woods to the left and climbs up steeply through bracken close to a fence with Private Property signs that encloses the quarry to the right. When the track levels off, take one of the paths to the left that leads after a short distance to the triangulation pillar (93m) at **Stone Hill** on Beeston Regis Heath. Here

The triangulation pillar at Beeston Regis gives a good view over Sheringham and the coast

there is a well-placed bench and an excellent view over Sheringham out to sea.

Returning to the main path along the fence continue to where the quarry boundary starts to curve south. Arriving at a signpost close to the fence, where several tracks run off in different directions, take the path that leads south just away from the fence, and then almost immediately follow the wide bridleway that leads east. This is marked with a post bearing the National Trust sign. Follow the track east through the conifers for half a mile or so, crossing several other tracks along the way. Further National Trust signs on posts mark the route.

The broad track continues next to a fence that eventually starts to veer right. Reaching a junction a little further on, take the path off to the left that leads through to the Norfolk Coast Path at an area of open heath at **The Roman Camp**. Turn right to follow the Norfolk Coast Path past a car park and caravan park. Cross Sandy Lane and continue along the waymarked Norfolk Coast Path

Circuiting Incleborough Hill near West Runton

turning left downhill along the road that is also sign-posted for a caravan site.

Beacon Hill, which includes Roman Camp, between Cromer and Sheringham, is Norfolk's highest point at 103 metres (338ft). This is part of a range known as Cromer Ridge, an old glacial moraine that marks the extent of the ice sheet at the time of England's last glacial period. Despite its name, there is no evidence of Roman settlement at Roman Camp although there are earthworks that are probably remains of a beacon dating back to the medieval period.

Arriving at the gates of the caravan park take the path to the right then, meeting a crossroads of tracks, walk left to leave the Norfolk Coast Path along a public bridleway. The path continues towards a wood where you take the second track to the left that leads around gorse-covered Incleborough Hill to the left. This narrows as it squeezes between hedgerows to approach a golf course. Cross the road that leads to the clubhouse and car park to take the track opposite that leads uphill next to a stand of conifers.

At the road, turn left then right along Calves Well Lane, which continues as a bridleway beyond the houses following the edge of woodland to eventually join up with the Norfolk Coast Path once more. This joins another track where you turn right north to walk towards the sea. ▶

The stretch of the Norfolk Coast Path that passes through Sheringham and Roman Camp lies close to the eastern end of the 45-mile (72km) Hunstanton to Cromer long distance route.

After passing **Beeston Hall School** turn left at the cottages along the service road to reach the A149 coast road. Cross the busy road and turn left and immediately to take the footpath that leads in the direction of the sea. Carefully cross the railway line. From here you can either continue straight on along the Norfolk Coast Path towards the sea, where it turns left to pass over the low hill before leading back to Sheringham promenade. Alternatively, you can take the path to the left just after the railway line, which joins a suburban road to lead back to the High Street and starting point.

WALK 18

Bodham and Baconsthorpe

Start	Bodham village hall (TG 126 402)
Distance	7½ miles (12km)
Time	3hr
Map	OS Landranger 133 North East Norfolk, Explorer 252 Norfolk Coast East
Refreshments	Pub at Bodham
Public Transport	Frequent buses to Holt and Sheringham
Parking	Bodham village hall

Central to this walk are the evocative remains of Baconsthorpe Castle, tucked away down little-used farm roads in the lush North Norfolk countryside. Despite being close to the North Norfolk coast, this walk passes through countryside of a very different character – quiet, sleepy and bucolic.

As some of the footpaths on this route may be quite overgrown later in the season, it is probably more enjoyable to walk this in the earlier part of the year.

Starting at Bodham village hall, next to the Red Hart pub, walk up to the main road. Turn left past houses and a bus stop to reach the Old School, and then turn left again, away from the road along a track marked as a public footpath. Go past allotments on the right to climb gently uphill with fields on the right and a mature hedgerow on the left. Climbing further uphill, a church becomes visible to the left before the track veers sharply to the right towards Manor Farm.

At the farm, turn left past cottages then cross the road to continue in the same direction along a marked footpath towards woodland ahead. The path drops gently to continue through a gap in the trees to reach a stile from where the ruins of **Baconsthorpe Castle** can be clearly seen ahead. Carry on along the right-hand side of the field to approach the buildings then veer slightly left towards the ruins at the top of the field. Go through the gate to walk past the moat and west side of the site

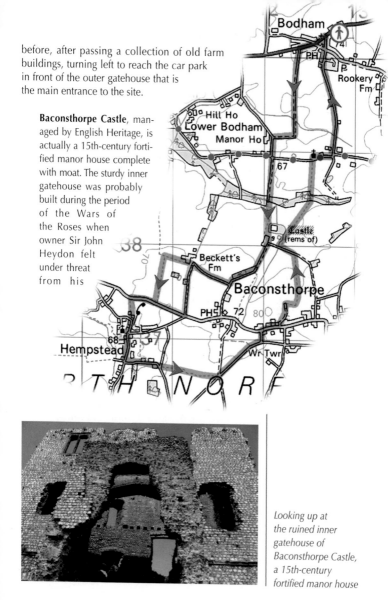

before, after passing a collection of old farm buildings, turning left to reach the car park in front of the outer gatehouse that is the main entrance to the site.

Baconsthorpe Castle, managed by English Heritage, is actually a 15th-century fortified manor house complete with moat. The sturdy inner gatehouse was probably built during the period of the Wars of the Roses when owner Sir John Heydon felt under threat from his

Looking up at the ruined inner gatehouse of Baconsthorpe Castle, a 15th-century fortified manor house

95

Old track climbing gently to Beckett's Farm near Baconsthorpe

enemies. His son Henry completed the fortified house, and the turreted outer gatehouse was added in Elizabethan times. Some of the buildings served as a wool processing factory during a prosperous sheep farming period in the 16th century but as the Heydon family fortune declined in the following century parts of the buildings were demolished to sell for building materials.

The outer gatehouse continued to be occupied until 1920, when one of its towers collapsed.

After exploring the site – an excellent spot for a picnic – go back out of the car park and turn right and left to take the track that leads south from the farm buildings. Ignore a left fork and shortly after turn right to take a track west towards **Beckett's Farm**. This track climbs gently uphill, affording views back to Baconsthorpe Castle and almost out to sea. Descend to some farm buildings, cross the road and follow the footpath ahead with the field on the left and hedgerow on the right. At the corner of the next field the path continues with a field on the right and hedgerow on the left. After a few minutes you meet another footpath that runs north–south: turn left along this to reach the Baconsthorpe to Holt road. Be wary of motor traffic as there is no verge or pavement here. Turn right. ▸

When the road bends around to the right, take the signed footpath that leads off left. This follows a hedgerow and eventually emerges on the main street of **Hempstead** village. Turn left to pass Chapel Lane and an attractive thatched church. Go past Hempstead Lodge then take the road to the left, signposted Plumstead–Aldborough, which is Marlpit Lane. Walk past flint cottages and soon turn left into a green lane then immediately look for the footpath sign in the hedgerow to the right.

Take the steps that lead up to the footpath which goes across an arable field towards the road ahead. Turn left at the road, ignoring a turn on your left, to reach Long Lane close to a **water tower**. Turn left to reach Baconsthorpe's old post office, where you turn right, and immediately opposite the Wesleyan chapel take the footpath that leads off left. Follow the field edges to continue north to emerge on the farm road close to **Baconsthorpe Castle**.

Go left along the lane a little way to reach a gate on the right and follow the footpath just to the right of Baconsthorpe Castle – there may be friendly, well-behaved horses in the field here. Go through a belt of woodland at the northeast corner of the field and then over a footbridge into another field and continue straight ahead in the same direction (north-northeast). At the end of the field the path enters Baconsthorpe Wood to emerge the other side in sight of the church ahead. Follow the hedgerow to reach All Saint's Church, then turn right at the road and left at the crossroads, from where the road continues north into **Bodham** village to return to the starting point by the pub and village hall.

Alternative route: the footpath beyond Beckett's Farm may be very overgrown in late summer. A worthwhile option is to follow the farm track south from the farm to join the Baconsthorpe to Holt road a little further east.

WALK 19

Itteringham

Start	Bure Valley Community Centre, Itteringham (TG 145 309)
Distance	5 miles (8km)
Time	2hr
Map	OS Landranger 133 North East Norfolk, Explorer 252 Norfolk Coast East
Refreshments	Pub and tearoom in Itteringham; tearooms at Mannington Hall
Public Transport	Weekly bus service to Aylsham, regular service from Holt and Norwich to Saxthorpe (3 miles away)
Parking	Community centre car park near St Mary's Church

This route links two sleepy villages – Little Barningham and Itteringham – by means of footpaths through land belonging to the Mannington Estate, one of several historic farming estates with grand impressive houses in north Norfolk.

Start at the community centre that lies just south of St Mary's Church on Rectory Road.

The graveyard of Itteringham's **St Mary's Church** has the grave of the poet George Barker (1913–1991). His gravestone is in the form of a granite book that bears the legend: 'No Compromise'. Graham Greene, who was an admirer of Barker's poetry, helped provide financial support during the years he lived in the village at Bintree House with his wife Elspeth.

Turn left and follow the track downhill crossing a stream. Shortly after turn right just before the track starts to rise uphill. This follows a hedgerow across fields with damp woodland off to the right.

Arriving at a cattle pen and a junction of paths, go left through the gates to follow a green lane that soon joins

Lush farming landscape near Itteringham

a farm track. Continue along the track, which swings around to the right next to **Mossymere Wood**. Pass a hedged garden and a house to continue north along Keeper's Lane and past a ruined farm building until reaching a road by Avenue Farm, a large complex of farm buildings. Turn right and then, after a short distance, turn left to cross the road to a track that follows a hedgerow to a plantation of trees ahead.

At the plantation – Oak Grove – follow the footpath to the right around the trees and then, at the corner of the larger Lady's Wood beyond, take the footpath left along the hedgerow to walk west towards the road. On reaching the road fork right to a footpath sign and then, after about half a mile of road walking, turn right at crossroads into **Little Barningham** village.

When St Andrew's Church on the hill becomes visible as the road begins to rise, follow the track to the right past Church Farm. At the house at the end, bear right to follow a green track beneath a steeply rising field to the left. At the end of the woodland, go through the gate on your right into a meadow and across a narrow field to go over a stile to reach the edge of Lady's Wood. ◄

Turn left to follow a narrow path, which may be considerably overgrown, along the edge of the wood and continue in the same direction to reach a broad farm track that eventually reaches a meadow. Arriving at a narrow belt of trees at the top of a short incline, turn right along the footpath that runs parallel to the plantation to head south.

Very soon, the impressive buildings of **Mannington Hall** come into view through the trees. Continue to reach a road and cross this to walk on in the same direction following the western edge of the plantation. This curves gently left to reach its southern edge where a footpath continues diagonally across the field towards the road and cottages at Kincardine.

> **Mannington Hall**, the home of Lord and Lady Walpole, is a 15th-century moated house built of flint and stone. Famous for its moat and walled rose garden, the hall is only open by special appointment but the gardens may be visited between May and August. No dogs are allowed except guide dogs.

Turn right at the road and, just before reaching the church, turn left along the footpath that follows the edge of a field. Dropping down to the road at the edge of **Itteringham**, turn right into the village passing a converted chapel and the community shop and tearoom along the way. Turn right at the junction by the telephone box and bus shelter to walk the short distance uphill towards the church and the walk's starting point. ◄

There is a broken signpost and stile here but this is not very visible.

Itteringham's village shop has been community-run since 2004. It has a café selling local produce that claims to be the smallest in the county.

WALK 20

Aylsham and Blickling

Start	Aylsham Market Place (TG 193 270)
Distance	7 miles (11.2km)
Time	2hr 45min
Map	OS Landranger 133 North East Norfolk, Explorer 252 Norfolk Coast East or Explorer 238 Dereham & Aylsham
Refreshments	Pubs and cafés in Aylsham and at Blickling Hall
Public Transport	Half-hourly bus service from Norwich and Cromer
Parking	Market Place, Aylsham

Circling north of the market town of Aylsham, this walk makes use of a section of the Weaver's Way long distance path to reach the extensive parkland of Blickling Hall before returning to the town by means of footpaths and quiet country roads.

Aylsham was the second town in Britain to be given 'Slow Town' status, earning the Cittaslow UK appellation in November 2004 to become a member of the international network of towns where life is considered to be good in terms of environment, infrastructure, urban fabric, promotion of local produce, hospitality and community.

The movement, which started out with the Slow Food interest group in Italy in 1999, and is led by Ludlow in the UK, has so far accepted just seven British towns into its ranks – Aylsham, Berwick-on-Tweed, Diss, Mold, Perth, Penarth and Cockermouth.

Starting at Market Place, go up past the Black Boys pub and turn right up Penfold Street. Arriving at the thatch-covered water pump, bear right, and at the next junction, where the Heydon road goes left, continue right along a

short section of the Blickling road that has no footpath.
Walk past Peterson's Road and then take the second of
two footpaths, signed Weavers' Way, which leads off left
opposite a large house.

This follows a broad track along an avenue of oak
trees that climbs gently uphill to reach a gate into a
farmyard. Ignore the footpath to the left that indicates
a Marriott's Way–Weavers' Way link route and take the
track to the right that skirts a field along a hedgerow. This

A wooden footbridge over the River Bure near Blickling

climbs a little more before levelling off and dropping down towards the houses of Silvergate ahead.

At **Silvergate** turn right along the road to walk through the hamlet and pass woodland on either side as the road climbs gently. Approaching the main road, the splendour of Blickling Hall comes into view ahead. At the road, opposite the church, turn left towards the Buckinghamshire Arms pub to pass in front of the entrance to **Blicking Hall** with its enormous topiary hedge. Bear right in front of the Buckinghamshire Arms and go past a barn and car park, bearing left along the road to arrive at Blacksmiths Cottage. Turn right here and walk past estate cottages to arrive at a white gate.

The current **Blickling Hall** was built in 1616, in the reign of James I, by Sir Henry Hobart. Before this, the earlier hall was in the possession of Sir John Falstaff, and later the Boleyn family, although Anne Boleyn may have been born in Hever Castle, Kent rather than here as is often claimed.

A property of the National Trust since 1940, the house is in splendid Jacobean style and its estate covers 4,777 acres, with 500 acres of woodland, 450 acres of parkland and the rest farmland.

▶ Follow the broad gravelled drive that leads north through the Blickling Estate. With the lake to your right,

Blickling Estate's park and woodland is open all year dawn to dusk. The house and gardens are open at more specific times and dates – see **www. national-trust.org. uk** or ring 01263 738030 for details.

pass a copse of ancient trees before going through a gate into a belt of beech woodland where the track swings around to the right. This continues around the north end of the lake. At the end of the lake, turn left along the path into the woods and follow this past a car park to reach a minor road.

Turn right past **Park Farm** then, after the second cottage to the right, take the path to the left that leads across a field to a footbridge. The path follows the wooden footbridge across the **River Bure** then leads right along the river bank a short distance before turning left away from the river along a line of trees. This continues through a kissing gate along a broader farm track between hedges and past farm buildings to reach a minor road.

Turn right at the road to leave the route of the **Weavers' Way**, which continues left. Follow this narrow, almost traffic-free, lane to loop south towards **Ingworth**. Just before reaching Ingworth, you join a busier road (The Street). Turn right to walk past the quaint thatched Church of St Lawrence on a mound to the left. Pass Banningham Road on the left to continue past a telephone box.

Leaving the village, take the public footpath to the left up a farm track opposite Woodside. This continues alongside a hedge to swing sharply right by power lines. Continue along here and after passing beneath power lines again turn sharp left to reach a kissing gate. Go through and along a meadow to emerge on the bend of a narrow road. Turn right to follow the road east and then south towards **Aylsham**.

The road passes **Abbot's Hall** in the woods to the left before going through **Drabblegate**, a string of cottages close to the river. Reaching the junction of the Banningham Road carry straight on, following the Weavers' Way sign over a bridge over the old railway line. Turn right at the main road to pass the turning for **Dunkirk** on the left to continue towards the town centre. Cross over the river at Millgate and up Gas House Hill to reach a junction. Turn left along Red Lion Street and then right to return to **Aylsham** Market Place.

WALK 21

*Old Hunstanton, Thornham and
Holme-next-the-Sea*

Start	Le Strange Arms Hotel, Old Hunstanton (TF 679 424)
Distance	12 miles (19.2km)
Time	4hr 45min
Map	OS Landranger 132 North West Norfolk, Explorer 250 Norfolk Coast West
Refreshments	Pubs in Old Hunstanton, Ringstead, Thornham and Holme, cafés in Old Hunstanton
Public Transport	Regular bus service to Cromer and King's Lynn
Parking	Car parks at St Edmunds Point and IRB Station, Old Hunstanton

This long circular route takes in one of the very best sections of the Norfolk Coast Path as well as chalk downs, rolling farmland and the spectacular cliffs at Old Hunstanton. The walk passes through the attractive coastal village of Thornham half-way round, an excellent place to break the walk and stop for lunch or a drink.

Begin at the Le Strange Arms Hotel near to the **lifeboat station** in Old Hunstanton. Walk uphill along Sea Lane towards the A149 Old Hunstanton Road then turn left. Follow this past The Old Coach House, Lodge Hotel and Waterworks Road on the left to reach Church Road on the right. Turn right and, before reaching St Mary's Church, go right along Chapel Bank to climb gently uphill to arrive at a corner with a bench. Turn left down Lovers Lane, the green track that leads between hedges off to the left.

The track soon opens out to give good views over the woodland of **Hunstanton Park** to the north. After about a mile the track veers left then right to skirt around **Lodge Farm**. Turn left along the minor road and then sharp right at the junction next to a semi-hidden pond to walk uphill along a farm track.

Reaching the top of the hill, the remains of a ruined chapel and a water tower can be seen across the fields to the right. The track then descends and swings

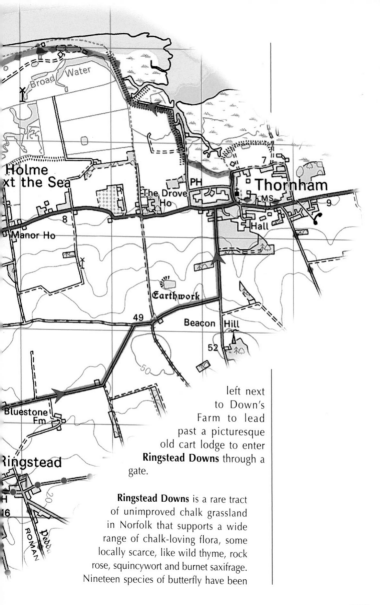

left next to Down's Farm to lead past a picturesque old cart lodge to enter **Ringstead Downs** through a gate.

Ringstead Downs is a rare tract of unimproved chalk grassland in Norfolk that supports a wide range of chalk-loving flora, some locally scarce, like wild thyme, rock rose, squincywort and burnet saxifrage. Nineteen species of butterfly have been

Old cart lodge at entrance to Ringstead Downs

recorded here, including the chalkhill blue and brown argus. The Downs are open access but walkers must keep dogs on a short lead March–July to avoid disturbance of ground-nesting birds.

Follow the path east through Ringstead Downs, past an exposed chalk cliff to the left to walk along a wide valley with a steep scarp to the left and a more gentle slope to the right. Walk through an area of woodland to climb slowly uphill before eventually reaching a sign that indicates a picnic area to the right. Continue straight on to reach a gate and walk on to reach the road.

Option: For a shorter walk, follow the Peddars Way to Holme-next-the-Sea, then turn left along the Norfolk Coast Path to return to Old Hunstanton.

Turn left to follow the road (and for a short time the route of the Peddars Way) through **Ringstead** village, ignoring the right turn to Docking just before the High Street. Walk uphill past the **pub**, shop and church to reach a road junction at the northern edge of the village. Turn right and continue heading east along Thornham Road where the Peddars Way leads off left towards the coast. ◀

Go past **Bluestone Farm** down in the valley on the right then follow the road left where it meets a field barn.

Bluestone Farm probably takes its name from 'bluestones' found in the area – glacial erratics, alien to the region, that were deposited by glaciers in the past.

Climbing gently uphill, the North Sea soon comes into view along with the tower of Holme church and a maritime wind farm. At the junction, turn right and at the next junction where there is a triangulation point and continue straight on east, heading downhill. Turn left at the next junction and follow the road past **Thornham Hall** into **Thornham** village.

At Thornham, turn right along the main road and then left at the bus shelter by the restaurant. Walk past the church on the right and Ship Lane to the left to reach a corner. Take the footpath ahead, which shortly turns left across a bridge to lead west across marshes with extensive reedbeds – the route of the **Norfolk Coast Path**. Arriving at the beach road, turn right and follow this for a short distance before climbing up the bank to the left. The path continues along this raised bank to head north then west past tidal channels and salt marshes filled with sea lavender. This continues west to go through a gate to enter the Holme Dunes NWT Reserve. The path follows a wooden walkway through the dunes towards a stand of pines, passing the entrance to Holme Bird Observatory.

Holme Bird Observatory was established in 1962 in the pine and scrub covered dunes near Holme-next-the-Sea. Its strategic position at a key migration point allows the study of various streams of migrants arriving or leaving the North Norfolk coast. Over 50,000 birds have been ringed since 1962 and more than 300 species recorded. A full time warden takes a census of the birds present each day and in spring a full breeding survey of the area is conducted.

Seahenge, an Early Bronze Age timber circle, was discovered on the beach close to

Spectacular cliffs at Old Hunstanton

Holme-next-the-Sea in 1998, when a low tide revealed a circle of timbers.

Option: Continue along the beach for 20 minutes from the turn to the lifeboat station for a good view of Old Hunstanton's spectacular chalk and red sandstone cliffs.

Continue through pines past paths leading to the beach to follow the walkway past a parking area. Where the walkway ends the path continues through **dunes** to eventually reach a golf course. Follow the Peddars Way sign to walk along a permissive path with the golf course on your left beyond a fence. At the end of the golf course, walk past a line of beach huts to reach a track off to the left that leads up to the **IRB Lifeboat Station**. ◄

Follow this past the lifeboat station to return to the Le Strange Arms Hotel.

WALK 22

Snettisham

Start	Snettisham, Rose & Crown pub (TF 686 343)
Distance	7 miles (11.2km)
Time	2hr 45min
Map	OS Landranger 132 North West Norfolk, Explorer 250 Norfolk Coast West
Refreshments	Pubs and tearoom in Snettisham
Public Transport	Regular bus service to Hunstanton and King's Lynn
Parking	High Street, Snettisham

Snettisham lies just inland from the west-facing coast of The Wash. This route leads to and from the sea, passing through forest, grazing marshes and sand dunes along the way. It also provides an opportunity to visit the bird reserve at RSPB Snettisham midway along the route.

From the door of the pub turn right along Old Church Road and then right again at the main road before going left along Alma Road past the Post Office. Walk past a road on the right up to Home Farm before taking the footpath to the right that leads diagonally across a field. Go over a footbridge and through trees to reach the A149 coast road.

Cross the busy road carefully (there is a central reservation a little further up to make this easier and safer) and continue along the track through the deciduous woodland of **Ken Hill Wood** ahead. The track climbs a little then flattens off in a more open area of pines to eventually turn sharp left before emerging at a gate from where there are clear views of the coast ahead. Turn right towards the buildings of **Lodge Hill Farm** and follow the path around the buildings to walk along a hedgerow towards the sea.

Carstone (or carrstone), a ginger-brown sandstone with a high iron content, is one of the principal building materials used in northwest Norfolk. Many

of the houses in Snettisham are constructed out of this local material, as are the buildings of other towns and villages in the region like Downham Market, Hunstanton and Wolferton.

Although many quarries used to exist in north-west Norfolk, only one at Snettisham now remains active.

The farm track turns sharply to the right and then left again before crossing a track that has No Entry signs – the track-bed of the old King's Lynn to Hunstanton railway line. Continue west towards the sea and where the track bears round to the left continue straight ahead to go through a field gate and over a dyke to continue across fields in the same direction. The path leads through a gap in the hedge and veers right to reach a signpost pointing left. Follow this towards the raised bank that is the sea

wall. Go through a stile and over a dyke, and walk around the northern end of a reedbed to reach the dunes with a clear view of The Wash and Heacham to the north. ▶

Walk left along the dunes to reach Heacham Dam, a reinforced walkway. Continue south to reach the beach and car park at **Snettisham Scalp**. The entrance to Snettisham RSPB Nature Reserve lies a little further on. Go across the car park to reach the road and turn left to pass **Shepherd's Port** and the entrance to a caravan park on the right, which has facilities like a chip shop, toilets and amusement arcade next to the road. ▶

Continue along Beach Road, heading inland past **Locke Farm** and Ken Hill Wood on the left. Walk past Common Road on the left and at the next bend take the track on the left that leads straight ahead to the main road. Cross the A149 and continue into Snettisham along Station Road, past carstone cottages and St Mary's Church Hall.

At the main road, turn left then right to continue in the same direction past bungalows and carry straight on along the cul-de-sac where it bends to the left. This soon joins a track, which climbs up and bends left towards the church past paddocks and the site of a Roman villa to the right. At **Park Farm**, go through a gate and continue

On a clear day at The Wash it is usually possible to see wind farms and 'Boston Stump', a tall and conspicuous church tower, across the water in Lincolnshire.

The best time to visit Snettisham nature reserve is between August and January, when up to 50,000 waders may be seen on the mudflats in front of the hides.

The Wash at Snettisham looking across to Lincolnshire

towards the impressive spire of St Mary's Church. Cross the road just before the church and follow Old Church Road around to the left to return to the walk's starting point.

St Mary's Church, Snettisham, a 14th-century spired church in Decorated style, is more typical of churches found in Lincolnshire than those in Norfolk. Nikolaus Pevsner has described St Mary's as 'perhaps the most exciting Dec (Decorated) church in Norfolk' but the church also has the distinction of being the first church in the United Kingdom to have suffered aerial bombardment, having being attacked and damaged by a Zeppelin airship in 1915.

WALK 23

Salthouse and Cley-next-the-Sea

Start	Salthouse, The Green (TG 074 439)
Distance	8 miles (12.8 km)
Time	3hr 20min
Map	OS Landranger 133 North East Norfolk, Explorer 251 Norfolk Coast Central
Refreshments	Pub in Salthouse, pubs and tearooms in Cley-next-the-Sea
Public Transport	Regular Coasthopper bus service to Hunstanton and Cromer
Parking	The Green, Salthouse

This highly rewarding walk delivers some classic North Norfolk coastal scenery – sand dunes, shingle banks, salt marshes, pebble beaches and reedbeds. It also gives a good taste of the North Norfolk hinterland, passing through heath, deciduous woodland and flinty agricultural land. The attractive coastal village of Cley-next-the-Sea, which lies halfway along the route, provides plenty of interest for its own sake as well as ample opportunities for refreshment.

Salthouse was once an important producer of salt, and evidence of salt production in the area goes back to Neolithic times.

Starting from the large triangle of grass by the main coast road known as 'The Green', walk east along the main road for a short distance and turn right up Grout's Lane opposite a bridleway that leads towards the sea. Follow the lane up to St Nicholas Church, going past Church Cottage into the churchyard. From the west side of the churchyard enter Cross Lane, which leads around flint cottages to join a road.

Walk uphill along the road past more flint cottages until reaching a footpath to the left that climbs up steps on a bank before crossing a field diagonally. Take this, and turn left on reaching a quiet lane. Follow this round to the right, ignoring the track ahead, to climb up Pinfold Hill. As the road levels out a little, take the footpath that lead off to the right along a farm track. This diverts from the farm track almost immediately to bear right through gorse to reach a more open area where the path divides. Follow the path to the left to walk through the gorse and heather of **Salthouse Heath** to reach an open area with birch trees and then a minor road.

> **Salthouse Heath**, just inland from the village, has earthworks from this period as well as several Bronze Age burial mounds. The heath is also of interest to bird watchers, with both nightingales and nightjars evident here in early summer.

Turn left at the road and go over a crossroads to head downhill past mature oak woodland on the right. Go straight across the next crossroads to pass through dense mixed woodland of oaks and beech. The road bends to the right, past Bixes Lane off to the left. Remain on the road, veering gradually west and going gently downhill to reach the Holt to Cley road.

Salthouse Heath, just inland from the village of the same name

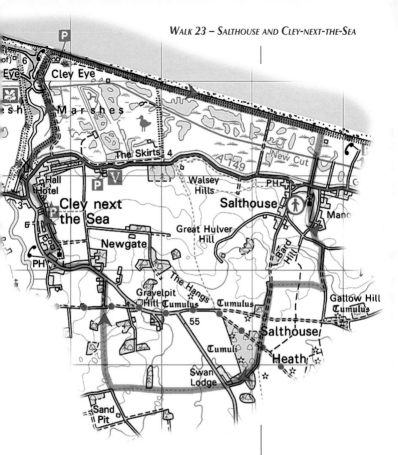

Go straight across to follow Hurdle Lane, a farm track that leads west along a hedge and the edge of fields. This climbs a little then levels off to continue as a green lane between hedgerows. The track descends past a wood to the right and narrows to become increasingly enclosed by the surrounding vegetation before emerging at the corner of a road. ▶ Turn right immediately to follow a farm track north along the edge of a flinty field. At the end of the field, go through a gap in the hedge to continue uphill towards a wood ahead. This continues through bracken

From here there are views north to the churches at Cley and Wiveton.

117

and scrub to reach Bridgefoot Lane. Go straight across to follow a hedge past Wymerhill Planatation to arrive at the road into **Cley**.

Turn left along the road, which is busy with traffic in summer, past Old Woman's Lane to the right and attractive flint cottage before reaching Cley's St Margaret's Church as the road curves around to the right. Walk past the church with the green on the left and next to the Three Swallows **pub** turn right along the footpath opposite the bus shelter. This narrow path goes past cottages and the pub garden to reach the rear of the church graveyard from where it continues to Church Road.

Turn left and follow the road down the hill past allotments and the village hall before taking the narrow path to the left between houses to arrive at High Street. Turn right, walk past the smokehouse and telephone box to reach Old Town Hall House where a sign indicates the route of the Norfolk Coast Path to the left. Follow this,

Iconic windmill at Cley-next-the-Sea, now a holiday dwelling

which turns right along a walkway behind the houses of Cley High Street.

Cley, pronounced to rhyme with 'eye', is no longer quite 'next-the-Sea' as its full title claims, although it was up until the 17th century when extensive land reclamation took place and the port consequently silted up. Before this time it was a busy port involved in the grain and cloth trade with the Low Countries. The village's St Margaret's Church, now several miles inland, used to sit right on the harbour.

The footpath continues next to reedbeds to reach Cley **Windmill**. Just beyond the mill, climb up steps to reach a path along a raised bank lined with Alexanders that runs through sea-lavender filled **Fresh Marshes** and alongside a minor road to reach the car park at **Cley Eye**. Turn right to follow the Norfolk Coast Path east along the shingle bank. This passes the marshes and pools of Cley Marshes NWT reserve to the left, one of the country's premier birding sites. ▸

Continue along the shingle bank towards Salthouse. After about two miles, a track leading across the marshes between two dykes leads to the main road just west of the village. Ignore this and take the next track, about half a mile further on, that leads right directly towards **Salthouse**'s St Nicholas Church. Follow this to the coast road then turn right to walk the short distance back to the starting point at The Green. ▸

Cley Marshes is of international importance for birdlife and has been a reserve in the care of the Norfolk Wildlife Trust since 1926, the oldest county wildlife reserve in the UK. Resident breeding birds include bittern, bearded tit, avocet and spoonbill, while winter visitors include large flocks of Brent geese and numerous waders. The marshes also receive many rare vagrants on passage migration making a highly popular destination for birders.

Depending on how clear the day is, it should be possible to see as far along the coast as the pines of Holkham to the west, and the cliffs of West Runton to the east.

The nearby Cley Marshes Nature Reserve visitor centre on the coast road is a modern, eco-friendly building with shop, adult education centre, viewing deck and a café offering superb views over the marshes

119

WALK 24
Blakeney and Wiveton Downs

Start	Blakeney Quay (TG 028 442)
Distance	5 or 6¼ miles (8 or 10km)
Time	2hr – 2hr 30min
Map	OS Landranger 133 North East Norfolk, Explorer 251 Norfolk Coast Central
Refreshments	Pubs and cafés in Blakeney, pub in Morston (slight detour)
Public Transport	Regular Coasthopper bus service to Cromer and Hunstanton
Parking	Large car park at Blakeney Quay

A circuit around the attractive coastal village of Blakeney that climbs inland to take in England's best-developed and well known esker, a geological feature from the glacial period, before returning to the tidal inlets and salt marshes of the coast. An optional loop at the end gives a further taste of north Norfolk's unique tidal creek environment.

Begin at the car park at Blakeney Quay. Turn right out of the car park and walk west along the quay before turning right across the green to take the footpath, signed Norfolk Coast Path, just beyond the village sign.

The Blakeney sign reflects the village's maritime heritage

Blakeney, like neighbouring Cley-next-the-Sea, is another north Norfolk village that used to be a commercial seaport before its harbour silted up. These days, only small craft can negotiate the route from the harbour out to sea past Blakeney Point. The village, which now serves mostly as an upmarket holiday resort, has two buildings of historic importance: a 14th century guildhall at the foot of High Street, and St Nicholas Church up on the coast road, which is distinguished in having two towers, the smaller of which is thought to have been a beacon to guide boats into Blakeney Harbour.

Walk past flint cottages to follow the path alongside **Morston Salt Marshes** in a westerly direction. Go past a footpath leading left and continue towards **Morston**, with the sand spit of Blakeney Point clearly visible to the right across Blakeney Channel. As Morston church and harbour come into sight take the bridleway that leads inland to the left. This threads past houses to join the coast road soon after. Turn right and then almost immediately left along a footpath that curves around the gorse-covered bank of a former quarry that has a thatched house perched above it.

Continue along the footpath south following a field boundary towards a copse of trees at **Kettle Hill**. Follow the field edge to the left to reach a fenced off area of woodland. The path continues around this to the right hand side before turning left at the corner of the plantation. Turn right at the next corner, where there is a house and garden, and walk along the driveway to reach a minor road. Go straight across this to follow the public footpath

The Norfolk Coast Path approaching Morston from Blakeney

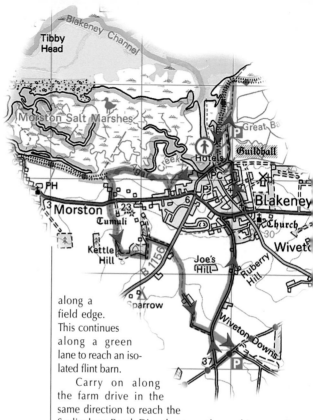

Tibby Head

Blakeney Channel

Morston Salt Marshes

P Great B

Hotels

Guildhall

PC

PH

3 Morston 23

Tumuli

P

6

Blakeney

Church

Wivet

Kettle Hill

B 1156

Joe's Hill

Ruberry Hill

30

along a field edge. This continues along a green lane to reach an isolated flint barn.

Sparrow

Wiveton Downs

37 P

Carry on along the farm drive in the same direction to reach the Saxlingham Road. Directly across the road is a permissive bridleway to **Wiveton Downs**. Take this through a scrubby area of heath and gorse. ◄ The bridleway (indistinct in places but just head roughly southeast) comes out at another minor road from where the permissive path continues past a car park. Turn right at the road, then right again at the crossroads to return to the Saxlingham Road entrance to Wiveton Downs.

Here are excellent views over Blakeney out to sea and the two towers of the village's impressive St Nicholas Church on the coast road.

Wiveton Downs is a local nature reserve and SSSI thanks to both geological and wildlife interest. Wiveton Downs is part of Blakeney Esker, a 3.5km sand and gravel ridge created by the laying down

Heath and gorse at Wiveton Downs above Blakeney

of sediment from meltwater rivers flowing under the ice sheet during the Quaternary period. The site is also rich in birds in summer, with linnets, stonechats, various warblers and sparrowhawks all frequent here, along with green hairstreak, peacock and painted lady butterflies. In winter, waxwings, short-eared and barn owls and hen harriers are sometimes seen.

Continue downhill along Saxlingham Road in the direction of **Blakeney**. Reaching the Blakeney road sign and the main road, turn right towards the church. Walk past the war memorial and just before the church turn left down Back Lane, the street just after High Street, into the village. Go past the ornate gateway into Whitefriars just before reaching the bottom and follow the road round to the left by the Manor Hotel. From here, either continue along the road to soon arrive back at the quay, or turn right along the restricted byway to the right, which follows a dike to reach the sea wall, before turning left to follow the Norfolk Coast Path south along the raised bank to return to the car park at Blakeney Quay. ▶

The path along the restricted byway to the sea wall can be very muddy and difficult to walk on after wet weather.

123

WALK 25

Little Walsingham, Houghton St Giles and
Great Snoring

Start	Coker's Hill Car Park, Little Walsingham (TF 933 369)
Distance	7 miles (11.2km)
Time	3hr
Map	OS Landranger 132 North West Norfolk, Explorer 251 Norfolk Coast Central
Refreshments	Pubs and tearooms in Little Walsingham
Public Transport	Regular bus service from Fakenham and Wells-next-the-Sea
Parking	Coker's Hill Car Park, Little Walsingham

This circuit follows well-trodden pathways for some of the way – Walsingham and its shrine has long been a place of pilgrimage for pious Christians of all denominations.

Even without the historical interest of Little Walsingham village itself, this is a delightful walk that climbs up both sides of the modest Stiffkey valley and offers fantastic views over a lush undulating landscape that on occasion is almost reminiscent of the Welsh borders.

From the car park walk down past the old mill building to reach Common Place, with its unusual 'pump' – a 16th-century pump-house with an iron brazier on top. The Tourist Information Centre and Shirehall Museum lie directly opposite, and the **Shrine** complex just beyond. Turn right down the High Street, past a gateway into the Abbey grounds on the left and tearooms on the right to reach Church Street on the left. Walk up Church Street over a bridge towards the church. Follow the road left around the church to reach a gate leading into the grounds of **The Abbey**, the ruined arch of the priory clearly visible beyond.

Walsingham, sometimes referred to as 'England's Nazareth', has been an important place of pilgrimage since the 11th century, when Richeldis de

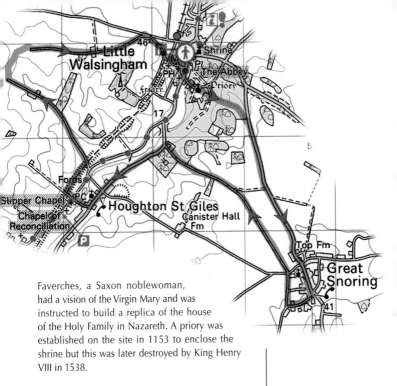

Faverches, a Saxon noblewoman, had a vision of the Virgin Mary and was instructed to build a replica of the house of the Holy Family in Nazareth. A priory was established on the site in 1153 to enclose the shrine but this was later destroyed by King Henry VIII in 1538.

Take the track immediately opposite that leads up past the graveyard towards farm buildings. Just before the farm buildings a footpath leads off to the left uphill to the left of a plantation of trees. Follow this, climbing uphill to reach a gate and stile, and go over this to arrive at the Little Walsingham–Great Snoring road just beyond a small copse of trees.

Turn right at the road and continue walking uphill past another copse of trees where a track leads off to the right (a potential shortcut if you do not wish to continue all the way to Great Snoring). As the road bends to the right the tower of **Great Snoring**'s church comes into view ahead. ▶

The road from Little Walsingham has a couple of blind corners just before it enters Great Snoring so take care on this stretch.

The Greenway to Walsingham from Great Snoring

Great Snoring, and its (slightly larger!) neighbour Little Snoring, take their unusual name from *Snarringes*, a Saxon name meaning the home of someone named Snear. In 1611, the then lord of the manor Sir Ralph Shelton sold the village to Lord Chief Justice Robertson, reportedly saying, 'I can sleep without Snoring'.

The Greenway between Great Snoring and Walsingham has been in use as a track between villages for the best part of a millennium and as a pilgrimage way for more than half this time.

Arriving at a crossroads by the social club and bus stop, continue straight on past flint cottages and St Mary the Virgin Church before taking the narrow footpath that leads right immediately after it. Follow this between walls to reach a shady graveyard and then continue past the Manor House, a very distinctive gothic dwelling that was constructed in the 15th century by the Shelton family. Turn right at the road then go straight across at the road junction to follow the signposted Greenway to Walsingham opposite, a broad, often muddy track that leads nearly all the way back to Little Walsingham. ◀

After meeting a track from the right (the shortcut from the main Little Walsingham–Great Snoring road) the path continues along a line of old oaks and open fields to the right. It then starts to drop more steeply, with good views ahead to the north. The greenway then drops to the bottom of a narrow valley before emerging at a road after passing woodland on the left. Turn left, following the road uphill to **Houghton St Giles**. At the crossroads, where a road leads down to a ford over the river, keep going past the church to take the next road to the right that fords the River Stiffkey and arrives at a corner next to the **Slipper Chapel**. ▸

The **Slipper Chapel** is a Catholic chapel just outside Walsingham at Houghton St Giles, built in 1340 as the last chapel on the pilgrimage route to Walsingham. It was customary to walk the last stage to the shrine barefoot and even King Henry VIII, who later destroyed the priory as part of the Dissolution, once performed this rite.

After the Reformation the chapel fell into disrepair and even saw use as an agricultural building

After a period of heavy rain the ford by the Slipper Chapel may be impassable on foot, in which case take the first ford just before the church as this should be easier to cross.

The modestly hilly landscape of northwest Norfolk near Houghton St Giles

until the late 19th century when it was restored by a wealthy local woman and re-established as a shrine.

Continue across the road, following the concrete farm track uphill a short distance before turning right onto the footpath that crosses it. This permissive path, which follows the route of the old railway line, now serves as the pilgrimage track between the Slipper Chapel and Walsingham, although the original route followed the road itself. Follow the pilgrimage track as far as a bridge then turn left down the steps to reach the track below and turn right to walk uphill along Stanton's Track, a permissive path that slowly climbs the western side of the valley. Follow this track past two plantations off to the right then, just after an isolated group of farm buildings on the left, take the path to the right that leads uphill along a hedgerow. This climbs up alongside two fields to arrive at Waterden Lane at more or less the top of a hill from where there are excellent views to the south and west.

Follow Waterden Lane east back towards **Little Walsingham**. Reaching another group of isolated farm buildings, continue in the same direction along a narrow track between hedges to arrive at a road. Bear right, then right again almost immediately afterwards to follow a steep, often muddy single lane road (signed No Through Road) downhill to emerge at the pilgrimage way/railway track opposite the former railway station building that is now the Orthodox Chapel of St Seraphim. Go straight on past the chapel then turn first left to return to the car park at Coker's Hill.

WALK 26

Brancaster Staithe and Barrow Common

Start	Jolly Sailors pub, Brancaster Staithe (TF 793 443)
Distance	4½ miles (7.2km), or 5½ miles (8.8km) via White Horse
Time	1hr 50min – 2hr 20min
Map	OS Landranger 132 North West Norfolk, Explorer 250 Norfolk Coast West
Refreshments	Pubs in Brancaster Staithe, café in Burnham Deepdale
Public Transport	Regular Coasthopper bus service to Hunstanton and Cromer
Parking	National Trust Activity Centre, Brancaster Staithe

This relatively short walk gives a good sense of the variety of landscapes to be found at the western end of the North Norfolk coast. Brancaster Staithe, with its creek and extensive salt marshes, is the haunt of weekend sailors; Barrow Common, just inland from the coast, is a gorse-covered expanse of heath with excellent views along the coast and out to sea, while Brancaster was once the location of a major Roman fort.

Facing the Jolly Sailors pub on the coast road at **Brancaster Staithe**, take the road to the right of it that leads inland. Walk up Common Lane, passing houses

Boats and cottage near Brancaster Staithe

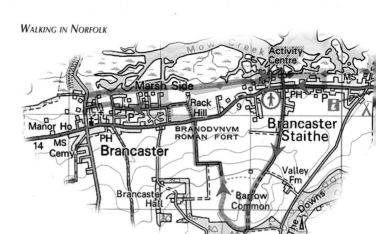

along the narrow road before reaching the top of the hill. Here, as well as an excellent view back out to sea, there is a sign for **Barrow Common** and paths leading both left and right. Continue along the road to reach the brow of

Heading down to the coast at Brancaster

the hill, where there is another track to the right and an open area to the left. ▶

Continue along the road as it starts to go downhill quite steeply then, just before joining another road from the left, take the public footpath that leads right, forking left when the path divides soon after. The path skirts through woods at the end of the common to climb slowly away from the woodland to follow the edge of the common as it swings round to the north along a wide grassy track. The sea comes into view again before a crossroads of tracks is met. Take the track to the left that leads north towards the sea past woodland.

Go through the gate and along a broad green track before turning left where it meets a farm track. Where the farm track swings left into a field continue straight on until it bends sharply right to head towards the sea. Follow this downhill all the way to the coast road.

At the road, cross carefully then go through a gate into the site of **Branodunum Roman Fort**. Go past the information board to reach the northeast corner of the field then walk left along the perimeter to arrive at a kissing gate. SSS Turn left onto a track and go over a cattle grid to join a road. Turn right to walk along Cross Lane past modern houses on both sides. At the end, turn right along Marsh Drove before taking the footpath to the left that is squeezed between two fields. This emerges next to flint and chalk cottages at London Street. Follow the street around the corner to the left along Butcher's Lane to reach a junction. Turn right and then right again when you come to the signed Norfolk Coast Path.

Barrow Common gives an excellent vantage point for a panoramic view of the North Norfolk coast.

The **Roman fort** of *Branodunum* ('The Fortress of Bran') was constructed in the third century AD to guard the approach to The Wash against Saxon invaders. It was built with a typical rectangular castrum layout, with four entrances and in Roman times its northern wall would have lain directly on the seashore rather than inland as it does now. There is some evidence that the site may have been used by Saxon settlers at a later date.

A multitude of signposts at Brancaster Staithe

This stretch of the Norfolk Coast Path passes an extensive reedbed to the left and runs along raised wooden boarding for much of the way back to Brancaster Staithe.

◀ Walk past the attractive flint houses of **Marsh Side** to arrive at the northern end of the Branodunum site. Leaving the houses of Brancaster behind, continue east along the wooden boardwalk as the creek of Brancaster Staithe comes into sight ahead. Shortly after reaching a converted barn, the path goes through a kissing gate towards flint cottages ahead. The path then skirts around a pair of cottages used as a National Trust **Activity Centre** to arrive at the car park at Brancaster Staithe creek. Continue towards a small harbour with fishing boats and a barn ahead. Here, there is an information board and a signpost that indicates the route of the coast path and the location of both of **Brancaster Staithe**'s pubs. Turn right to return to the main road and the Jolly Sailors. ◀

Option: continue along the coast path for half a mile to the White Horse, then return to the starting point along the main road.

4 CENTRAL NORFOLK AND BRECKLAND

A sunny woodland ride in Thetford Forest

WALK 27
Thompson Common and Pingo Trail

Start	Car park just off A1075 between Watton and Thetford (TL 941 966)
Distance	7½ miles (12km)
Time	3hr 15min
Map	OS Landranger 144 Thetford & Diss, Explorer 237 Norwich
Refreshments	None on route. Pub in Thompson
Public Transport	Regular bus service from Watton and Thetford to Stow Bedon, a mile and half from start/end point
Parking	Thompson Common car park

This is a walk that skirts the edge of the MOD 'Battle Area' of Stanford Training Area and takes in a variety of Breckland habitat – heaths, wet woodland and commons. The route also passes the 'pingos' of Thompson Common, considered to be landscape remnants of the last Ice Age, and makes use of both a disused railway line and a quiet stretch of the Peddars Way. The wildlife is excellent on this walk and, in addition to plentiful birds, plants, butterflies, dragonflies (and mosquitoes!), there is a very good chance that deer – roe and muntjac – may be seen.

Some of this route goes through very muddy terrain, always worse after prolonged wet weather, so appropriate footwear is essential. Note that dogs may be walked on the Peddars Way and the old railway line but not on Thompson Common Nature Reserve.

From the car park, which is just set back from the main road, take the track that leads south past a farm on the left and woodland on the right. This straight track, once part of the old Swaffham to Thetford railway line, which closed in 1965, leads through a conservation area and then woodland on either side before traversing more open land at **Crow's Meadow**. At Crossing Keeper's Cottage, go across another broad track to carry on in the same direction past **Sandpit Plantation** and through **Breckles Heath**.

This continues through **Cranberry Rough**, an area of very wet, almost swamp-like woodland with muddy ponds full of yellow flag irises on either side of the track.

Dragonflies and butterflies are plentiful here in summer, as are hungry mosquitoes. ▸

In summer, mosquitoes can be a nuisance, especially through damp areas like Cranberry Rough, and insect repellent is strongly advised.

Cranberry Rough was once a large lake, the product of the melting glaciers of the last Ice Age. The lake was an important source of fish and wildfowl from the Neolithic period until Tudor times, when it was known as Hockham Mere, and it only silted up to become a swamp as recently as the 18th century. The site, which is now a SSSI, provides very rich wetland habitat for many plants, birds and insects, and over 60 species of spider have been identified here.

After Cranberry Rough the track reaches an old railway cutting. Take the steps to the right that climb up onto **Hockham Heath**. Go through a gate in the fence, turn left and then follow the path around to the right alongside a conifer plantation. At the road, turn right and then, reaching a junction to the left, continue along the road past signs warning of the military **Danger Area** to arrive at a fork in the road.

Bear right to follow the track and the way-marked route of the **Peddars Way**. The track continues past woodland and open areas of grazing to reach a track to the right signed to **Watering Farm**. Carry straight on until the watery expanse of **Thompson Water** becomes visible

Coniferous forest and sheep grazing beside Peddars Way near Thompson Water

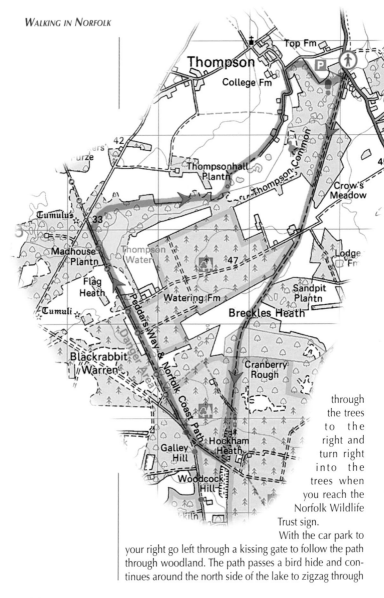

through the trees to the right and turn right into the trees when you reach the Norfolk Wildlife Trust sign.

With the car park to your right go left through a kissing gate to follow the path through woodland. The path passes a bird hide and continues around the north side of the lake to zigzag through

*Thompson Common
with its Ice Age
pingos*

woodland before reaching a T-junction with another track. Turn right to follow the track through a hazel coppice and across a dyke. Turn left after crossing to follow the path parallel to the dyke on its right hand side. The path continues through the damp alder, oak and hazel woodland of Thompson Carr alongside the dyke for some distance before reaching a bridge back across the dyke that leads through a gate to an area of open meadow, **Thompson Common**, with marker posts ahead indicating the way ahead to the northeast.

Go through a gap in the hedge at the end of a meadow then over a gate to follow the track signed 'Pingo Trail'. Continue along the side of fields to the left and hedge to the right.

> **Pingos** are mounds of earth-covered ice normally found in the Arctic and subarctic areas like northern Canada and Siberia where permafrost exists. Those found in the Breckland area of Norfolk are thought to be pingo ruins – the pond-like depressions that remain after the pingos collapsed when the ice thawed at the end of the last Ice Age.

The larger pingos lie just to the right of the trail – shallow ponds edged with reeds and sedge. This path joins a farm track to pass a wooden barn and houses, which twists left, right, and then left again after crossing a stream. Just before a Give Way sign, take the track to the right that leads through woodland and over bridges and past more ponds to emerge at the car park at the starting point.

WALK 28

Swannington and Upgate Common

Start	St Margaret Church, Swannington (TG 134 193)
Distance	4 miles (6.4km)
Time	1hr 45min
Map	OS Landranger 133 North East Norfolk, Explorer 238 Dereham & Aylsham
Refreshments	None on walk
Public Transport	Nearest regular bus service is to Attlebridge, two miles south, which has frequent buses to Norwich and Fakenham
Parking	High Street, Swannington

This short but rewarding walk takes in a typical yet varied tract of unspoiled central Norfolk countryside, passing along an intriguing and historic green lane and over two commons rich with wildlife en route.

Swannington has an ornate thatch-roofed water pump dated 1888 that was erected in memory of Hastings Parker and his wife Elizabeth who lived at the Manor House.

◄ Starting from **Swannington** High Street, walk up to St Margaret Church and turn right down Church Lane. Walk past the buildings of Hall Farm and **Swannington Hall**, with its crow-step gables, to follow the road around the corner to the right and continue past rough grazing meadows and The Woodlands before reaching farm buildings ahead. Turn left through a gate to follow a farm track leading east that gives good views to the south, then take the signed track to the right that leads due south

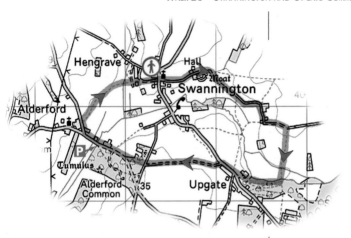

along a shady, almost entirely enclosed sunken green lane known locally as Swiffer's Lane.

> **Swiffer's Lane** – or 'Swift Foot' Lane as it was also known – was once reputedly used as an escape route for smugglers who, coming ashore at the Norfolk coast, divided up their bounty at a farm in nearby Cawston, a well known smugglers' haunt. Swiffer's Lane was just one the tracks they supposedly made use of for a fast getaway.

Near the end of the lane, it leads along a wooden walkway through damp woodland before crossing a footbridge over a shallow stream. Where the path ends, take the right turn along a wooden walkway parallel to the stream to pass through the woodland of Upgate Common.

> **Upgate Common** has had SSSI (Site of Special Scientific Interest) status since 1981. The common has a good range of habitats within its relatively small area of 20 hectares: dry and wet acidic heath, fen, birch and alder woodland, rough grassland and

*Sheep grazing near
Swannington*

ponds. The open fen area on low-lying ground has plants such as meadowsweet, marsh cinquefoil and southern marsh orchid, while its ponds are home to several species of amphibians including the scarce great crested newt (*Triturus cristatus*).

This emerges at an open area of common land just before the houses of **Upgate**. Turn right along the road to pass the village sign and a post box before taking the footpath to the left just after the derestricted speed limit sign. This follows a farm track between fields and towards woods ahead. Arriving at the road, take the footpath opposite that leads straight ahead into the woods of **Alderford Common**. This drops steeply down a bank to start with before levelling off before coming to a road.

Turn right to walk for a little less than half a mile along the road. Go past cottages and over a small stream to pass Bell Farm on the right. At the junction, just before the church at **Alderford**, turn right and then right again along a public footpath across a field.

Continue with the hedgerow on your right before veering northeast a little to follow the path. Go through a gap in the fence over a small footbridge and then over a larger one to continue through Hengrave Common towards the buildings of **Hengrave** ahead. At a T-junction of paths, turn right past a pond and along a farm track to the right of Manor Farm. Joining the driveway to Swannington Manor shortly afterwards, turn right and walk up the drive to arrive at the road back in front of Swannington's St Margaret Church.

WALK 29

Hockering

Start	Victoria pub, Hockering (TG 073 130)
Distance	5 miles (8km)
Time	2hr
Map	OS Landranger 133 North East Norfolk, Explorer 238 Dereham & Aylsham
Refreshments	Pub in Hockering
Public Transport	Half-hourly bus service from Norwich and King's Lynn
Parking	Hockering High Street

Although the entire length of this walk takes place fairly close to the busy A47, the route outlined here includes a peaceful riverside path through woodland, footpaths along the edge of ancient woodland and deserted farm tracks. This is central Norfolk scenery at its best, although it may be muddy and wet underfoot in places.

Walk west from the Victoria pub past the garage, Post Office and Manor Farm with its impressive barn and crow-step gabled house. Cross the busy A47 using the staggered crossing and turn down the road that lies just ahead, signposted to Mattishall. Walk down Mattishall Lane past woodland on the left to drop down to a valley. Just after a minor road from the right, take the sign-posted

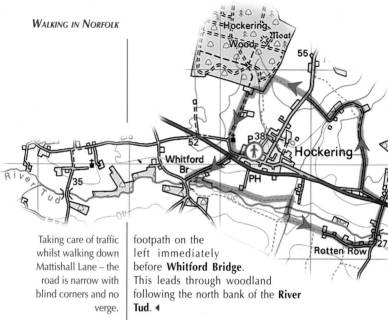

Taking care of traffic whilst walking down Mattishall Lane – the road is narrow with blind corners and no verge.

footpath on the left immediately before **Whitford Bridge**. This leads through woodland following the north bank of the **River Tud**. ◄

The River Tud, a tributary of the Wensum, meanders east near Hockering

The **River Tud**, a tributary of the River Wensum, flows for just 14 miles from its source near East Dereham to its confluence at Hellesdon Mill near Norwich. Fast-flowing and clear, it is rich in aquatic life like crayfish and freshwater shrimps and is prized by local anglers for its dace fishing.

Follow the path that runs parallel to the meandering river, which can be surprisingly fast-flowing after wet weather. The path threads through shady alders and over numerous small footbridges to continue east. Reaching an open area, the track veers off across a meadow to the left away from the river. It continues through a belt of trees and through grazing meadows, often wet underfoot, to arrive at a track by a modern barn.

Carry on in the same direction through the gate with a waymark sign to follow a farm track. This climbs gently and then splits, although both tracks rejoin a little further on. Go over a stile to follow a hedge on the left until, just before arriving at a fence, the track bends sharply right to reach a footbridge over the River Tud. Crossing to the south bank, follow the footpath south over two stiles and walk diagonally across the corner of a field to reach another stile. Follow the path across the next field and then through a hedge towards the buildings that can be seen ahead.

Walk past the converted farm buildings of Riverside Farm to follow the lane that leads past the cottages of **Rotten Row**. At the bottom turn left to head to cross the river once more and climb back up towards the A47 – the last section of this road is narrow with a blind corner, so take care. At the junction with the main road, rather than going straight across up Sandy Lane, take the minor road to the left that leads uphill and veers gradually away from the main road. This passes an old milestone with the legend: 'Norwich 9 miles, Dereham 7 miles'. Turn right at the top of the hill along the hedged farm track that leads between fields and climbs gently to give good views over what is typical central Norfolk farming landscape.

The edge of Hockering Wood, a large tract of ancient woodland in central Norfolk

Follow the track as it curves sharply left and drops down to the valley bottom. Continue south past the buildings of Coney Beck on the left and woodland on the right before arriving at a corner where the main track turns sharply to the right. This climbs up past fishing lakes towards a road where a line of semi-detached council houses are visible from some distance. On arriving at the road, take the footpath opposite that follows to the left of hedge all the way to **Hockering Wood** ahead.

> **Hockering Wood**, privately owned but open to the public, is designated an SSSI and one of several tracts of ancient woodland in Norfolk. The principal tree species is small-leaved lime, bluebells carpet the woodland floor in spring and a large number of moth species occur here.

Turn left at the edge of the wood and follow the path as far the corner where, rather than continuing along the track ahead, turn right along the wood's southern edge towards the farm buildings ahead. At the farm yard, turn left along the track towards **Hockering**'s church. Arriving at the church, enter the churchyard to find the footpath that leads through the hedge at its southeast corner. This leads along a fence to reach the road. Turn left to pass Manor Farm and arrive back at the Victoria pub.

WALK 30
Shipdham

Start	Shipdham All Saints Church (TF 958 074)
Distance	4½ miles (7.2km)
Time	1hr 45min
Map	OS Landranger 144 Thetford & Diss, Explorer 237 Norwich
Refreshments	Café and pub in Shipdham
Public Transport	Regular daytime bus service to East Dereham and Watton
Parking	The Green, Shipdham

This short figure-of-eight walk takes in the large village of Shipham and some typical central Norfolk countryside of arable farming on flat, relatively high land.

Shipdham is one of Norfolk's largest villages. Stretched along the main road halfway between the market towns of East Dereham and Watton, it also lies close to the geographical centre of the county.

The village served as the first US heavy bomber base with B-24 Liberator bombers during World War II. The airfield still exists just east of the village and is now privately owned. The village's All Saints Church, which dates from the 12th century, has an unusual wood and lead spire on top of its short tower that is a 17th-century addition.

Go down Mill Road directly opposite the church, walking south along it until reaching a road junction from

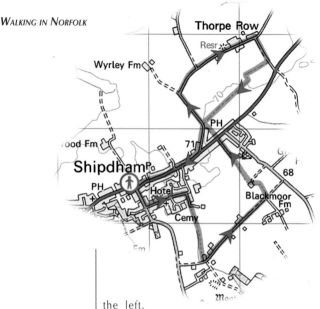

the left.

Turn left along
Pound Green Lane, past a chapel and **cemetery**, to
reach a footpath leading off along Watery Lane to the
right. Turn right along this and, at the corner where the
road swings left, continue in the same direction along
the edge of a field next to a stream. At the next field this
switches to the other side of the hedge before emerging
at a quiet lane. Turn left along the lane to pass farm cottages and continue along this for a little less than a mile
to reach the entrance to a farm on the right just before
a road junction.

Just beyond the drive to **Blackmoor Farm** to the right
take the footpath to the left, leading across a field towards
an isolated farmhouse. Walk around the buildings to the
right then turn left and right to take the footpath that continues northwest across another field opposite the farmhouse. This emerges at a track that leads to the main road
ahead next to a chapel. Cross the road, then turn left and
immediately right along the footpath by a hedge to pass
allotments.

At the end of the allotments by the corner of a road turn right to follow the road up past a turning to **Wyrley Farm** on the left. Follow the road around to the right, past open fields to the left and wet meadows to the right, and at the next junction take the right turn towards the farm buildings at **Thorpe Row**. Pass a raised grassy mound to the left (a **reservoir**) and continue past the farm buildings to reach another minor road off to the right.

Turn right to follow this until reaching a bridleway to the right just before the main road. Take this to follow it across fields directly towards the allotments and the spire of Shipdham's All Saints Church that can be seen ahead. Once back at the corner next to the allotments, turn left at the road and then right onto **Shipdham**'s High Street. Follow the street past a shop, garage, fish and chip shop and post office to return to the starting point by the church.

Old cottages tucked away down quiet central Norfolk lanes near Shipdham

WALK 31
Santon Warren and Thetford Forest

Start	Santon Downham Forestry Office (TL 816 878)
Distance	7miles (11.2km)
Time	3hr
Map	OS Landranger 144 Thetford & Diss, Explorer 229 Thetford Forest in The Brecks
Refreshments	None on route. Drink vending machine at Grimes Graves visitor centre and pubs and cafés in Brandon
Public Transport	Regular bus service from Thetford and Brandon
Parking	Santon Downham Forestry Office car park

A walk in Thetford Forest that begins and ends just south of the Little Ouse River in Santon Downham, a forest village that is actually in Suffolk although most of the walk takes place within the Norfolk boundary.

Virtually all this walk is off-road, along forest rides and footpaths, some of it following parts of the St Edmund Way. The route also skirts Grimes Graves, a Neolithic flint mining complex.

Santon Downham is a small village just over the Suffolk border that mostly revolves around the forestry business. The village used to be part of the Downham Hall estate but the hall was demolished in the 1920s as forestry took over the area, and most of the buildings in the village date form this time or later. Santon Downham was almost entirely overwhelmed by drifting sand in the 17th century as a consequence of severe erosion in this region of light sandy soils. The village now serves as the base for the Forestry Commission's East England office.

Walk out of the Forestry Office car park and turn left at the road to go over a bridge spanning the Little Ouse River. Continue along the road, climbing a little, to pass a road on the right before reaching a railway line. Take the track to the left that runs parallel to the railway line, just south of it. Follow this until reaching an underpass, then turn right, underneath the tracks, and then left to follow the railway line on its northern side. This track is not so well defined but it

eventually meets up with a broad track close to where rail signals are on the line. Look for a broad, long woodland ride that leads off north to the right and follow this uphill through the trees.

Where the track splits, take the right hand turn that bears left almost immediately to continue in the same northerly direction. Where another track crosses at a sharp angle, take the track to the right that leads northeast to reach a broad open track. Cross the track and continue along a less well-defined path next to a line of gorse bushes. This ends at a fenced off area – the southern perimeter of the **Grimes Graves Flint Mines** site. ▶

The mounds on the other side of the fence are the remains of the many flint mines that were worked in this flint-rich area in the Neolithic period.

149

GRIMES GRAVES FLINT MINES

Grimes Graves, in what is now Thetford Forest, is an extensive flint mining complex of over 400 mine shafts up to 14m deep and 12m wide, dug into the chalk to reach seams of flint beneath. The site is believed to have been worked during the Neolithic period between 3000BC and 1900BC, although mining probably continued well into the Bronze and Iron Ages.

Flint was of fundamental importance in the Neolithic period for the manufacture of stone axes, as the smelting of ores for metal had yet to be discovered. The mining method was very labour-intensive and required considerable manpower to remove the surface chalk before stone could be extracted. The hand tools most widely used were picks fashioned from red deer antlers. Grimes Graves is currently managed by English Heritage, with a shop, picnic area and exhibition at the visitor centre. Visitors are also able to descend into one of the shafts to see the flint seam below.

Thetford Forest ride, with open heath to the left

Turn right to follow the perimeter fence as far as a stile and gate. Go over the stile and take the broad track off to the right. ▸ Follow the track away from the fence, ignoring another track that leads off right, and continue more or less east through forest and open areas of heath to eventually emerge at a minor road. Turn right and walk along it past a large house and **Field Barn**.

Follow the road past the house around a corner to the right and along a short straight stretch to meet a track crossing the road. Turn left, then immediately right along a narrow track that soon widens out. Follow this past the first broad track that crosses it to reach a second. Turn left here past a track to the left, then go over three crossroads of tracks as the main track descends gradually before heading uphill again. Meeting an intersection of five tracks where the main track turns left up towards a main road, take the track that leads off sharp right. This leads past **Blood Hill Tumulus**, a prehistoric mound that has an interpretive board besides it.

The track continues downhill to emerge through trees at Hereward Way, a broad track that runs parallel to, and just north of, the railway line. Turn right, heading downhill to pass Largling Hill, the site of former church and holy well, where a short detour along the grassy boundary bank is worthwhile for the view down to the valley and the buildings of **Little Lodge Farm** below. Continue along Hereward Way to reach cottages to the left where the path swings left underneath the railway line before turning right again.

Straight ahead is All Saints **Church**, sometimes called 'St Helens', a tiny flint church with an octagonal tower. Either walk right along the path through the picnic area or, if you wish to examine the church more closely, go down to the road in front of the church and walk right. Either way, you soon come to the car park and toilet block of St Helen's Picnic Site. Go over the meadow in front of the car park to reach the footbridge over the Little Ouse and cross it to return to the Suffolk bank. ▸

Continue straight ahead through the wood after the bridge then follow the way-marked St Edmund Way

If you wish to visit the Grimes Graves site, continue along the perimeter fence bearing left at the corner – it is about a mile to the entrance and visitor's centre.

The Little Ouse River, a tributary of the River Great Ouse, defines the Norfolk–Suffolk border for much of its 37-mile (60km) length.

151

The Little Ouse River near Santon Downham marks the Norfolk–Suffolk boundary

between paddocks. Turn right along the edge of woodland and stay on the main track when another leads off to the left. Follow this gently uphill through woodland to reach the **Santon Downham** road just before the village road sign, turn right and follow the road to reach St Mary's Church by the village green. Turn right to return to the Forestry Office car park.

5 WEST NORFOLK AND FENS

The round tower of St Mary's Church at Beachamwell is of Saxon origin and one of the oldest in Norfolk

WALK 32

Harpley and Peddars Way

Start	Rose and Crown pub, Harpley (TF 788 258)
Distance	7½ miles (12km)
Time	3hr
Map	OS Landranger 132 North West Norfolk, Explorer 250 Norfolk Coast West
Refreshments	Pub in Harpley
Public Transport	Hourly bus service in daytime from Fakenham and King's Lynn
Parking	Nethergate Street, Harpley

Beginning and ending at a quiet west Norfolk village. this circuit takes in an attractive stretch of the Peddars Way as it passes through 'High Norfolk'. This is complemented with a loop through the beautiful woodland of the Houghton Estate and finishes with a little road walking along quiet, virtually traffic-free lanes.

Facing the Rose and Crown pub on Nethergate Street, turn right to pass the bus stop and village hall to reach Brickyard Lane. Turn right and follow the track that continues past a playground to reach a bench where a narrow footpath continues in the same direction. This soon emerges at open fields to join a wider farm track. Follow the farm track that continues in the same direction between two hedges – this may be very muddy in places. This leads towards a main road ahead but before reaching this take the sign-posted grassy track to the left that descends quite steeply between tall hedges down to the valley bottom.

Harpley derives its name from the old English words hearpe and leah and means something like 'harp-shaped clearing' or 'harp-player's clearing'. Until recently much of the village's land was owned by the Marquess of Cholmondely, whose residence is at nearby Houghton Hall. At 88 metres above sea level it is one of the highest villages in Norfolk.

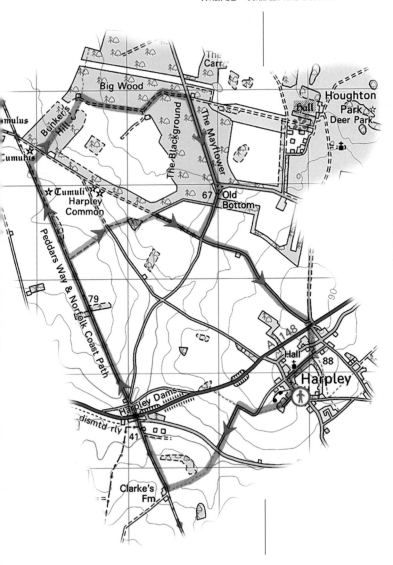

The Peddars Way, which links with the Norfolk Coast Path at Holme-next-the-Sea, is Norfolk's principal long distance footpath. It starts at Knettishall Heath in Suffolk and was originally a Roman road.

Optional route: follow the bridleway northeast downhill from the Peddars Way just before Harpley Common. Turning right at the minor road and follow this all the way back to Harpley.

Cross the road at the bottom and then continue along the footpath in the same direction. This passes an area of woodland to the right before following the edge of a field along a hedgerow towards a house ahead. On reaching a broad track – the Peddars Way – at **Clarke's Farm**, turn right to follow it as it climbs gently uphill past mature oaks. This soon levels off to drop down again to the A148 road just a after a quarry and a car park to the right. Carefully cross the road and continue along the lane opposite. This soon reaches a junction of five roads. Take the one directly opposite, next to Harpley Dams Cottages: this soon becomes a green lane once more. ◄

The **Peddars Way and North Norfolk Coast Path** climbs uphill for the next half a mile or so from here. Eventually it levels off, to give excellent views of the west Norfolk farming landscape on both sides. Where the hedge and fence finishes at a more open area, a track leads off to the right to drop down towards woodland. This offers a shorter alternative route back to Harpley if desired. ◄

Continue along Peddars Way with the expanse of **Harpley Common** to the right to pass close to a grassy

Bronze Age tumulus on Harpley Common seen from Peddars Way

tumulus visible to the right. Just before converging with the road, a permissive path leads over a stile across Harpley Common to the right, just south of another tumulus. Take this, heading across the common to the stile on the right next to car parking area at the edge of woodland. Go over the stile and across the road to take the footpath that leads through the trees to climb **Bunker's Hill**. ▸

The tumuli of Harpley Common are Bronze Age burial mounds – several more are found in the area.

The path climbs up through mixed woodland and swings right and then left again to continue in a northerly direction. When it reaches the edge of the wood continue across the open grassy area to the isolated cottage opposite. At the cottage turn right to follow the track along the edge of **Big Wood** towards the farm buildings ahead. After passing a large woodland ride to the left the path swings left in front of the entrance to the farm complex and continues along a broad farm track with a wide verge and trees on both sides. There may be large stacks of timber piled here ready for transportation.

Turn right at the road opposite the gatehouse of **Houghton Park** – the road may be fairly busy but it is straight, with a wide verge for walking if necessary. Turn

The edge of Big Wood at Bunker's Hill

right at **Old Bottom**, where the main road curves left towards the houses of Houghton village. Take the first lane to the left. This quiet lane climbs gradually past some isolated farm buildings to swing gently right. Just before the main road look for a signpost in the hedge to the right. Take the footpath over the stile that leads half-diagonally across the field towards buildings ahead to reach another stile on the other side. Carefully cross the A148 and take the footpath immediately opposite that leads across a field to the left of farm buildings. At the road turn right and then left along a track to arrive at another road by a triangulation pyramid (88m) with good views ahead to the south. Turn right to go downhill along Church Lane past St Lawrence's Church. Arriving at the village sign on Nethergate Street, turn left to go past a converted Methodist chapel and arrive back at the pub and your starting point.

WALK 33

Tittleshall and Godwick

Start	St Mary's Church, Tittleshall (TF 894 211)
Distance	4 miles (6.4km)
Time	1hr 45min
Map	OS Landranger 132 North West Norfolk, Explorer 238 Dereham & Aylsham
Refreshments	Pub in Litcham 2 miles (3.2km) south
Public Transport	Very occasional buses from Fakenham and King's Lynn
Parking	Tittleshall Church

Tittleshall lies close to the former medieval village of Godwick, where a ruined church and the foundations of the village's houses may still be seen. This walk crosses a landscape of extensive farmland and woodland to reach the deserted village in an evocative setting in 'high' west Norfolk south of Fakenham.

Tittleshall, of Saxon origin, is distinguished as being the second highest village in all Norfolk.

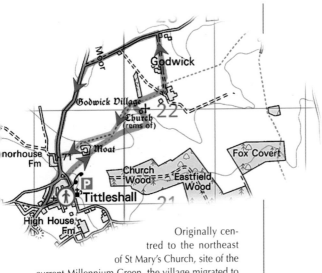

Originally centred to the northeast of St Mary's Church, site of the current Millennium Green, the village migrated to its present location in the 16th century. The village manor was bought by the Coke family in the late 16th century along with the land surrounding the nearby deserted village of Godwick. It remained part of the Holkham Estate until 1958, when it was sold to pay death duties. A brick manor house – the predecessor of the Coke seat that is now at Holkham Hall – was built close to the deserted village and monuments to Sir Edward Coke and other members of the family stand in Tittleshall's 14th-century St Mary's Church.

Facing the church, turn left to walk a little way along the road past Millennium Green towards a triangular intersection. Just before reaching this, look for the footpath signpost in the hedge that may be hidden by vegetation and go over the small footbridge into the field. Walk diagonally following the footpath across the field, aiming for the far edge of the copse of trees that is marked as a **moat** on the map. ▶ On reaching a farm track, turn

If the footpath has been ploughed over, an option is to follow the edge of the field east then north to reach the farm track by the copse of trees and moat.

Ruined church tower at deserted medieval village of Godwick

right towards the **ruined churchtower** that is now clearly visible ahead.

Walk towards the tower to reach the next hedgerow that marks the boundary of the old medieval village and where an interpretative board gives information about its history. Cross the footbridge and go through a stile into the extensive site, which is grazed by sheep. The ruined church tower lies diagonally to the left and a large barn, formerly belonging to the Coke estate, can be seen ahead. Exploring the site, several signs dotted around give details of the history of **Godwick village**. Godwick Great Barn, built around the same time as the manor house that was demolished in 1962, is now sometimes used for wedding receptions and there may be evidence of this if visiting on a weekend.

Godwick village, mentioned in the Domesday Book, was populated until the 17th century but poor harvests and wet weather had seen it decline gradually over the previous two centuries. The medieval village of 15 or so householders, together with a church, mill and a millpond, ran for about a quarter of a mile along a single street.

The original church was pre-Norman but the tower that remains today is not part of that church although materials may have been used from the older building. The remaining earthworks are a Scheduled Ancient Monument under the auspices of English Heritage

Having finished exploring the site, head for the fence at the north of the site and join the footpath that leads east to the hall and modern buildings of **Godwick's Hall Farm**. Turn left along the farm track and follow it past another group of buildings, now a B&B, to reach a junction. Turn left along the minor road and continue until reaching the main Fakenham to Litcham road. Turn left and follow this

Sheep graze on the land that was once Godwick medieval village

(there is a grass verge) until reaching Manorhouse Farm and the Tittleshall village sign.

Bear right into the village at the triangular intersection and then sharp left at junction onto High Street. Go gently uphill past a Methodist chapel and a bowling green to arrive back at the church and starting point.

Alternative

To avoid much of the road walking, simply return from the Godwick village site by following the path that leads southwest on the other side of the site boundary fence. This continues past the north side of the wooded moat to emerge at the edge of the village opposite Manorhouse Farm.

WALK 34
Helhoughton and West Raynham

Start	All Saints Church, Helhoughton (TF 869 265)
Distance	4 miles (6.4km)
Time	1hr 45min
Map	OS Landranger 132 North West Norfolk, Explorer 238 Dereham & Aylsham
Refreshments	None on route but pubs and cafés in Fakenham
Public Transport	No regular bus service
Parking	Helhoughton High Street

This pleasant, short walk leads through the upper reaches of the River Wensum and takes in part of the Raynham Estate, with its magnificent house and farm buildings. In addition to some fine pastoral west Norfolk countryside, a bonus is the ruined but still occasionally functioning church of St Mary's at West Raynham.

From **Helhoughton** High Street follow the small lane that leads south immediately opposite All Saints Church. At the last of the houses, go left over a stile into the field where a broad track continues in the same direction. ▶ Follow the track, which soon swings around to the left to pass woodland on either side, before crossing the river. Go through a kissing gate and turn right to see the farm buildings of the Raynham estate up ahead. The upper reaches of the **River Wensum** are now to your right, although the water itself may be difficult to see thanks to the height of vegetation on either bank.

Arriving at the farm buildings go through a gate to enter the farmyard of a large working dairy farm. Walk up through the farmyard past an impressively large complex of cattle sheds and stables to go through a gate over a cattle grid past cottages with crow-step gables. Bear right along the road through a paddock area with lime trees, the edge of **Raynham Park**, towards the church. Very soon, the elegant edifice of **Raynham Hall** can be seen to

The ruined church at West Raynham can be clearly seen ahead.

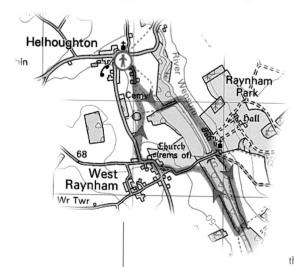

the left up the hill. Go past the gatehouse to reach the road and turn left.

Raynham Hall, built of brick and stone in Italianate style in the early 17th century, is the seat of the Townshend family. Charles 'Turnip' Townshend (1674–1738), who introduced the four-field rotation method to British agriculture, was born here and also spent his later years here carrying out agricultural experiments. The hall is also the scene of one of the most famous ghost photographs ever produced – 'The Brown Lady of Raynham Hall' – in which an ethereal shape, said to be the ghost of Lady Dorothy Walpole, was captured descending a staircase by *Country Life* magazine photographers in 1936.

Almost immediately, a footpath sign leads through trees away from the road. Take this and follow the footpath that emerges from the trees along the edge of a field next to a marshy area. The path continues with a large arable field rising up a hill to the left and damp woodland to the right.

After about half a mile at a field corner a signpost points to the right into the wooded area. Take this track, which leads to a footbridge over the River Wensum, narrow at this upper reach of its course. After another footbridge and stile, turn right to walk north with the woodland on your right. There may be cattle in the fields here

Estate cottage of flint with crow-step gable at Raynham Hall

that need to be circumvented but otherwise continue north over stiles and footbridges to reach a meadow that needs to be crossed diagonally away from the trees up towards a raised bank to reach a lane.

> The **River Wensum**, which takes its name from an Old English word for 'winding', is one of Norfolk's principal rivers and a tributary of the River Yare. Its source lies just east of the Raynhams, close to Whissonsett. It flows east through Norfolk, passing through a number of villages before reaching Norwich, where it becomes navigable between New Mills Yard and its confluence with the River Yare at Whitlingham. The whole length of the river is designated as an SSSI.

Turn left along the lane lined with lime trees. As the road bears round to the right it is possible to make out Raynham Hall and the church in the distance once more.

St Mary's Church at West Raynham is still sometimes used for outdoor services

The Church of St Mary's at West Raynham, although roofless, still has a font and altar and is occasionally still used for outdoor services in fine weather.

Swinging to the left, the road reaches a junction that has a village sign for 'The Raynhams'. Turn up to the right past a chapel to reach The Street and turn right again past **West Raynham** village hall and reading room. Just off to the right lies the ruined yet well-maintained **Church** of St Mary's, which is well worth a look and offers a peaceful spot for rest and refreshment. ◄

Leaving the village, just after a play area, a footpath leads off to the right after the road swings to the right around a corner. Follow this to cross a field diagonally and reach a farm track in the next field. Continue in the same direction to join up with the track that you set out on when first leaving **Helhoughton**. Go through the stile to the left at the bottom of the lane and walk the short distance north back to Helhoughton's High Street and All Saints Church.

WALK 35
Castle Acre

Start	Ostrich pub, Castle Acre (TF 816 152)
Distance	7½ miles (12km)
Time	3hr
Map	OS Landranger 132 North West Norfolk, Explorer 236 King's Lynn, Downham Market & Swaffham
Refreshments	Pub and tearooms in Castle Acre, pub in Newton
Public Transport	Occasional buses from Swaffham
Parking	Stocks Green, Castle Acre

For a relatively small, isolated village, Castle Acre has plenty to offer: in addition to being a picture-perfect rural idyll, it also boasts a Norman motte and bailey castle, a Cluniac priory and a large parish church.

The surrounding countryside is undulating with excellent views over west Norfolk, and both the Peddars Way and Nar Valley Way pass through the village. Nearby, the small thatched Saxon church at Newton serves as a reminder that the local population were God-fearing individuals well before the Norman invasion dramatically changed the look of the landscape.

Castle Acre is best known for its Norman ruins – a Cluniac priory and a motte-and-bailey castle. Both were founded in the late 11th century by William

Gatehouse to Cluniac Priory, Castle Acre

de Warenne, the first Earl of Surrey soon after the Norman Conquest. The village was formerly a fortified town and the 14th-century Bailey Gate that still stands is evidence of this.

Facing Stocks Green, with the pub behind you, turn left and then right to pass through the 14th-century **Bailey Gate**. Walk down Bailey Street and turn left just before a converted Methodist chapel. This leads through a gate to reach the **castle remains**. Skirt the castle mound then go over a footbridge and up steps before descending in the same direction to

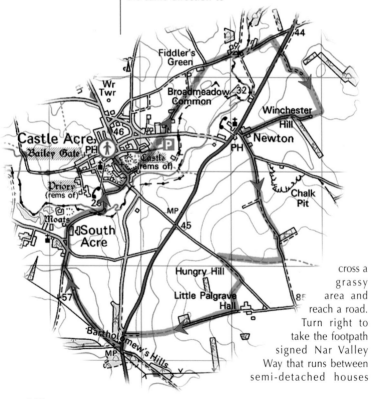

cross a grassy area and reach a road. Turn right to take the footpath signed Nar Valley Way that runs between semi-detached houses and open fields with watermeadows below. At the corner, where the path turns left, keep straight on across a meadow to reach a gate in the fence at a road. Cross the road to walk up the track opposite signed 'Unsuitable for Motors'.

Go past cottages to walk up to **Broadmeadow Common**, bearing right where another track converges to follow a shady lane between fields. This emerges by a house to merge with a metalled lane. Continue in the same direction until reaching a group of flint cottages, where the lane splits. Turn right over the bridge to cross the River Nar by an old mill building then immediately left to reach more cottages, where you take the green track that skirts them to the right. Before reaching the main road turn right on a footpath that leads across the field to the right. Follow this to reach steps that climb up to the busy A1065. Cross the road to walk up the farm track opposite that slowly climbs up **Winchester Hill** alongside a hedgerow.

The track levels off to arrive at a field corner where a public footpath sign points right. Turn right to follow

Looking down to the Saxon tower of All Saints Church at Newton-by-Castle Acre

another farm track where, as you drop down, the distinctive tower of **Newton**'s All Saints Church becomes visible below. At the bottom, walk past a three-storey farmhouse to arrive at a junction. The church is just to the right now, across the main road.

> **All Saints Church** at Newton-by-Castle Acre is one of the oldest in the county, of Pre-Conquest Saxon origin and with many surviving Saxon features such as its short central tower and arches. Most of the windows are a 14th-century replacement and the distinctive continental-style cap on the tower is probably another later addition.

Turn left at the road junction to walk uphill away from the main road and, where the road divides, take the right-hand turn. This quiet lane climbs up past a large **chalk pit** towards a copse of trees on the hilltop. Once beyond this, turn right along the track that crosses the road. This runs alongside a field edge to give excellent views to the north, where the buildings of Castle Acre soon come into view in the valley below. The track skirts the edge of a wood to emerge at a narrow road. ◀ Turn left to walk uphill before taking the bridleway to the right just before the farm buildings at **Little Palgrave Hall**. The track turns left to pass a pond before reaching a metalled farm track.

Here a shorter option would be to turn right to follow the road for a mile and a half back to Castle Acre.

Turn right along the track and where it ends at a plantation of trees continue in the same direction along the edge of fields down to the A1065 ahead. At the main road cross and, rather than taking the road immediately opposite, walk left a little way to reach another road on the right – the route of the Peddars Way into **South Acre**. Turn right and follow this to reach a crossroads, where you take the narrow road to the right that says 'Deep Ford'. Follow this downhill past farm buildings to the ford, where there is a footbridge over the River Nar and a good view of the **Priory** to the left. ◀ Continue along the road and take the next right, Blind Lane, to emerge at the bottom of Bailey Street. Turn left to walk up the road through the gate and return to your starting point.

The ford should be avoided after long periods of heavy rainfall as the road may be so flooded that the footbridge is inadequate for crossing the river.

WALK 36
Roydon and Roydon Common

Start	Three Horseshoes pub, Roydon (TF 707 228)
Distance	7 miles (11.2km)
Time	2hr 30min
Map	OS Landranger 132 North West Norfolk, Explorer 250 Norfolk Coast West
Refreshments	Pubs in Roydon and Congham
Public Transport	Regular bus service from King's Lynn
Parking	In Roydon village, at Chequers Green, or at Roydon Common on Lynn Road

Although this walk begins and ends in a quiet Norfolk village, much of the route is through spectacular heathland - a taste of what much of the west Norfolk countryside would have looked like in the pre-enclosure period. Surprisingly for East Anglia, the scale and apparent wildness of the landscape here can bring to mind upland regions like the Peak District or even the Scottish Highlands.

With the Three Horseshoes pub behind you, turn right to walk a little way along the main road past the telephone box. Take the lane to the left just after a junction to the right. Turn right at the bottom and follow the road past bungalows to reach a T-junction at Chapel Road. Go straight across and through the gate opposite to follow a broad green track that continues in the same south-westerly direction. This follows a deep ditch with a brook to the left and woodland to the right.

Continue through another gate past a wet area known as Hudson's Fen on the right. After another gate, the track eventually merges with the path of the old railway line. Continue past a more open scrubby area to the right to reach another gate that leads onto a road to the left. Take the track off to the right past the white house. This leads west through an often waterlogged area with the conifers of Grimston Warren on the left. Climb gently

Roydon village sign showing the King's Lynn to Hunstanton railway that used to serve the village

uphill to arrive at a large open area off to the right – **Roydon Common**.

Although ancient grazing areas such as Roydon Common used to dominate this part of the county the vast majority of west Norfolk's commons and heaths were forested or put under the plough as a result of Parliamentary enclosure. Roydon Common is now the largest surviving area of open heath in west Norfolk. Carefully managed by Norfolk Wildlife Trust by means of carefully controlled grazing, this has been a National Nature Reserve since 1995. Specialist plants here include bog asphodel, bog myrtle and cranberry, while nightjar, snipe and nightingale are just some of the scarce birds found here. In winter, hen harriers, merlins and short-eared owls may also be seen.

Roydon Common near King's Lynn, a National Nature Reserve manage by the Norfolk Wildlife Trust

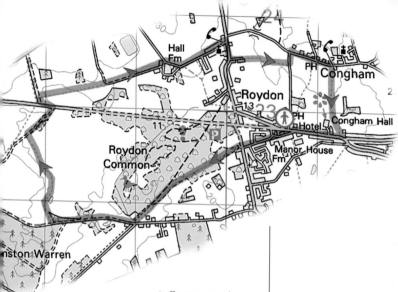

▶ Go past a marker post indicating the Grimston Warren grazing area and continue along the broad track that marks the southern edge of Roydon Common. This passes through an area of woodland before emerging at a more open area to climb gently uphill next to the boundary fence. Soon a large tower becomes visible ahead to the left – a World War II observation tower for ordnance practice. Passing a gate to the left and a track leading south in the direction of the tower, look for the path to the right that leads north across Roydon Common. Follow this through heather and bracken towards a large solitary pine.

Continue past the remains of pits and quarries off to the left. Meeting another broad track, turn right to go past information boards. Go through a gate with a sheep grid, then through a car parking area to arrive at a road. Turn left along the minor road and then right along a footpath next to a stand of pines. After about 100m, turn right again to follow the footpath along a hedgerow with a large arable field to the left. This climbs gently to reach a plantation of conifers on the left where the path continues along a broader track in the same direction.

On older maps, Grimston Warren is marked as an area of coniferous woodland. This is no longer the case as the area has been cleared and managed by the Norfolk Wildlife Trust to allow it to revert to its original heathland habitat.

The track levels off then descends down towards the buildings of Hall Farm ahead. Pass a large modern barn to the road and turn left in front of the farm buildings and then right along Church Lane. Keep going past Rectory Close and All Saint's Church to reach a junction. Turn right past the Roydon village sign, a bus shelter and a footpath to the right that leads to the church.

Take the track off to the left that leads past modern houses and, at the end, cross into the field to the left to follow the hedgerow in the same easterly direction. This climbs uphill with the road bridge of the old railway track clearly visible across the field to the left. At the field corner turn left along the track to soon reach the Congham road next to the junction with Broadgate Lane. ◀

Follow the main road past the village sign into Congham, walking past the Anvil pub and Keepers Lane on the left before turning right after a line of cottages along the farm track that is waymarked to Congham Hall. Follow this alongside a hedge to pass Congham Hall on the right and continue through the car park along the drive to reach the main Grimston to Roydon road. Turn right to pass flint and carstone cottages to soon arrive back at Roydon's Three Horseshoes pub.

Close to Hall Farm, just after Church Lane swings round to the right, a footpath to the right leads directly back to Roydon – this offers a slightly shorter alternative route back to the starting point.

WALK 37
Narborough and Nar Valley

Start	All Saints Church, Narborough (TF 747 130)
Distance	8 miles (12.8km)
Time	3hr
Map	OS Landranger 132 North West Norfolk, Explorer 236 King's Lynn, Downham Market & Swaffham
Refreshments	Chinese restaurant in Narborough, pub and tearooms in Castle Acre (5 miles away)
Public Transport	Bus service to Norwich and King's Lynn
Parking	All Saints Church, Narborough

This enjoyable walk takes in a peaceful and scenic section of the Nar Valley Way along the south bank of the river of that name. Almost entirely off-road, either alongside the river itself or along farm tracks and bridleways, the route also passes through Pentney village before returning to the starting point in Narborough.

With the church behind you, turn left to walk north along the main road. Pass the gatehouse to **Narborough Hall** across the road, and the converted stone chapel that serves as a Heritage Centre, to turn left down River Close, where a signpost indicates the Nar Valley Way. At the end of the close, take the footpath that leads off left next to a hedge. This soon turns right to pass along the bottom of gardens before heading left again along a channel that soon joins the south bank of the River Nar. Continue along the path on the river bank to follow the Nar Valley Way west. ▶

The Nar Valley Way is a 34 mile (54km) long distance path entirely within the watershed of the River Nar that runs between King's Lynn and Gressenhall near East Dereham.

Across the river can be seen a large complex of buildings that was formerly a malting and, shortly after, is a series of concrete supports, still in place across the river, that used to support the railway line that crossed

The water wheel that once belonged to a bone mill on the River Nar near Narborough

here. From here, the river and path meander a little to pass a poplar plantation before arriving a sluice and, on the opposite bank, a large defunct waterwheel that used to belong to Narborough Bone Mill.

Narborough Bone Mill once marked the limit of navigation of the River Nar upstream from the port of King's Lynn. All that remains today of the mill, which dates from the early 19th century, is the cast iron waterwheel and a few brick foundations. This isolated mill once took in bones from local slaughterhouses as well as large quantities of whalebone, a by-product of King's Lynn's once-thriving whaling industry. Human bone exhumed from north German cemeteries is also said to have been brought here for grinding down into fertiliser.

The bones were brought from King's Lynn by barge and the mill's relatively remote location was probably chosen in consideration of the powerful aroma that must have been emitted. With the arrival of the King's Lynn to East Dereham Railway in 1847, bone meal was taken by barge upriver from here to Narborough Maltings from where it was unloaded for the short journey by horse and cart to Narborough Station. For more information on Narborough Bone Mill and details about open days look at www.bonemill.org.uk.

Further on, the track reaches at a small brick building and a bridge across the river that has tracks leading off right and left. Continue past Marham Gauging Station and its **sluice**, and a track leading south to **Marham Fen**. ◄ Pass another farm track off to the left before going through a

The view opens up here, with open fields to north and south and a single hedgerow on the left.

gate. After a relatively straight section the river meanders a little more and the buildings and priory of Abbey Farm can be seen to the north across the river.

The river turns sharply right next to a sign for the Nar Valley Way. Where the river turns sharply left soon after, leave the

The tranquil River Nar west of Narborough

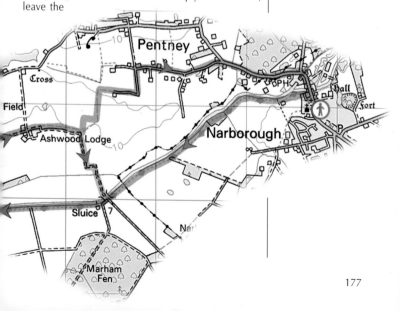

Nar Valley Way to cross the footbridge to the other side of the river and take the footpath to the right that leads to **Abbey Farm** and its **ruined priory**.

> **Pentney Priory gatehouse** at Abbey Farm is all that remains of an Augustinian Priory that used to be located here, one of three Augustinian complexes in the Nar Valley. The priory was established in the early Norman period by Robert de Vaux, a Norman noble who came to England with William the Conqueror.
>
> The three-storey gatehouse, built in the late 14th century of flint and limestone, is a smaller version of that found at Thornton Abbey in Yorkshire. Following its dissolution in 1537, much of the stone used for Pentney Priory has been reclaimed for use in several farms and domestic buildings in the Pentney area. The restored gatehouse is now used for holiday accommodation and as a wedding venue.

Reaching the gatehouse, follow the footpath to the right that skirts the edge of the farm and continues along the edge of a tall Leylandii hedge. Just before reaching a fence, go through the gap in the hedge to emerge at the bottom of a camping field. Turn right through the trees to reach a gate with a footpath sign and turn left. The path continues through a gate to follow a farm track along the edge of fields.

An alternative return route from Ashwood Lodge, avoiding road walking altogether, is to continue to the river, cross the sluice and retrace the riverside walk back to the start.

Arriving at a large man-made rectangular pond surrounded by a fence continue along the farm track to head towards trees and farm buildings ahead. The track swings sharply left and then right to continue towards **Ashwood Lodge**. At Ashwood Lodge, carry on through the farm buildings and go past a road to the left that leads north to **Pentney** village. Continue in the same direction along the farm track through open fields until arriving at a sharp bend to the right. ◀

Leave the track to turn left along the bridleway towards Pentney church in the distance. Turn right at the next field to follow the edge of a field next to a ditch. At the next corner, go through to the adjoining field and turn left along the field edge. Follow this, turning right at the next corner, to eventually arrive at some semi-ruined farm buildings.

Take the farm track to continue east and then north towards **Pentney**. Turn right at the crossroads by a carstone house and follow Low Road, a quiet country line, past a carstone cottage and a wooded area to reach a road. Turn right along Pentney Road, passing a large area of woodland and the old railway station cottage to the left, before arriving at the old maltings complex that is now an industrial estate. Turn right at the main road next to the Ship Inn (now a Chinese restaurant) and the Narborough village sign. Go over the bridge opposite another converted mill complex to return to the starting point by the church.

WALK 38

Beachamwell

Start	The Green, Beachamwell (TF 751 053)
Distance	7 miles (11.2km)
Time	2hr 45min
Map	OS Landranger 143 Ely & Wisbech, Explorer 236 King's Lynn, Downham Market & Swaffham
Refreshments	Pub in Beachamwell
Public Transport	No regular bus service
Parking	Parking spaces on Old Hall Lane in front of The Green, or on grass by the Village Hall (**do not** park on The Green – it is a fineable offence)

Beachamwell is a quiet village on the edge of the Norfolk Brecks that is picturesquely arranged around a large green, where the village's ancient thatched church takes pride of place. This walk takes in two more very evocative ruined churches in the locality and follows a length of charming green lane as well as bridleways, farm tracks and woodland paths. There is also a limited amount of trudging across fields.

Facing The Green, with the pub behind you, walk towards St Mary Church, with the village hall and a line of cottages to your left.

Beachamwell used to be made up of two separate manors – Bicham (or Bycham or Bilcham), which had St Mary's as its parish church, and Wella (or Welle), which had All Saint's. The two manors joined in 1568 to form the single village known today as Beachamwell. There is some dispute locally whether or not the village should be spelled Beechamwell, with two 'e's. Significantly or not, beech trees are plentiful in the locality.

St Mary Church, Beachamwell is mentioned in the Domesday Book and has a Saxon round tower that is one of the oldest in Norfolk, dating from the early 11th century. The tower is topped with an octagonal belfry, a later addition. The church is that last of four churches that used to serve the area when it was more populous in medieval times.

At the last of the cottages take the footpath that leads left along the edge of a field behind houses. Ignoring another footpath that leads diagonally right across a field, keep to the path along the bottom of gardens and, reaching a gate into a field to the left, go through this to continue in the same direction with the hedge on the right. Approaching Hall Barn ahead, veer left across the field to join Old Hall Lane. Continue past the entrance to Hall Barn and go through a gate to follow a grassy track to the scant **ruins of All Saints Church** ahead.

St Mary's Church has pride of place at the village green at Beachamwell

All Saints Church, abandoned in the 17th century, is almost totally ruined with just fragments of flint walls remaining. St John, northwest of the village, although it was actually abandoned earlier, in the 16th century, is a little more complete, with a square tower still standing. The fourth of the churches in the area is St Botolph's in neighbouring Shingham, a tiny Norman church which is now redundant and in private hands, although its churchyard is still in use.

Take the path southwest from the church ruin to reach a gate. Follow the path that continues across a field to reach a marker post where another footpath leads sharply right in a northerly direction. ◄ Walk north, with the ruined church and Old Hall to your right across the field. Cross a field boundary and then continue over the next field to reach a hedgerow.

Note that the path may be indistinct here when crops are more mature.

Turn left here to follow the hedge west to reach a minor road. Turn left and then right at the first junction, where it is signed to Barton Bendish and leads towards a wood. Follow this very quiet road, known locally as Murgot's Lane, past the southern end of the wood – Murgot's Covert. Go over a small stream and continue gently uphill. After passing a track to the left, take the broad track that leads right over a low bank shortly after this. ◄

This is Green Drove, which, like Murgot's Covert, is a county wildlife site.

Follow Green Drove between tall hedges of hawthorn and blackthorn to slowly climb uphill alongside power lines. The path soon broadens out as it flattens off further on. Beyond where the power lines end the

The ruins of St John's, a former parish church

track narrows somewhat to be flanked more closely by the blackthorn hedge before it reaches footpaths that lead right and left. Turn right and follow the path along a hedgerow as the ruined tower **of St John's Church** comes into view ahead.

Cross the farm track to go over the stile into the field that contains the church – there may be horses here – and after exploring the ruins follow the path diagonally southeast past a pond and copse of trees to reach the corner of the field. Go over a stile and follow the path between fields to reach a road. ▸

Turn left at the road and follow it past the buildings of **St John's Farm** to reach another road. Turn right and then left shortly after to follow the track opposite the driveway to **Beachamwell Hall**. Follow this towards a large wood ahead and, reaching the edge, take the path to the right that runs parallel to the west of the trees.

Continue in the same direction past the end of the wood and, arriving at an intersection of paths, take the one to the right along a field edge that follows the right hand side of a stand of trees. Cross the road and continue in the same direction past another wood and paddocks to emerge at a road. Turn left past white cottages to reach the hamlet of **Shingham**.

Reaching a road to the left, that has cottages along it and a drive to the right, that leads to Shingham Old Rectory, take the signed footpath to the right that leads through a gate to cross diagonally between paddocks. This goes over a footbridge before entering an area of woodland with nest boxes and plenty of woodpecker activity. At the edge of the wood, the path continues west along a green track towards the houses of Beachamwell ahead before emerging next to the **pub** in front of The Green and St Mary Church.

A short cut can be made from St John's Church ruin by turning right at the road, and then left to return directly to Beachamwell.

WALK 39

Hilgay Fen

Start	Rose & Crown pub, Hilgay (TL 621 987)
Distance	4 miles (6.4km)
Time	1hr 40min
Map	OS Landranger 143 Ely & Wisbech, Explorer 228 March & Ely
Refreshments	Pub in Hilgay
Public Transport	Regular bus service from King's Lynn and Downham Market
Parking	Along road at East End, Hilgay

This short walk around a pretty village on the edge of The Fens incorporates a short but idyllic section of the River Wissey as well as peaceful (and muddy) bridleways and footpaths alongside bird-rich woodland.

The bridleway leading past Hilgay Fen is often used by tractors and consequently is often very churned up and muddy underfoot.

From the corner of Bridge Street, close to the Rose & Crown pub, turn left along East End. Walk along this and continue straight on along the bridleway at the corner where Church Road leads off to the right. This follows a green lane between hedges with rough grazing meadows off to the left. The bridleway continues east alongside **Hilgay Fen** to a point where it turns sharply right then left again to reach a more open area with large oaks and other mature trees beside the bridleway.

Arriving at a point where the track bends gradually around to the right, take the bridleway through a gate into a field to the left. This follows a raised bank that bends round to the right before reaching the south bank of the **River Wissey**. ▶

> **Hilgay Heronry**, a small copse of mature European larch and ash trees close to the River Wissey, is a nationally important breeding colony of grey herons that has an average of about 40 occupied nests each year. The two-hectare site was awarded SSSI status in 1985.

Follow the river bank right towards a large brick building ahead. As you progress, the pastoral beauty of the scene is diminished a little by the sight of a large sugar factory emitting smoke in the distance. Go through a gate and turn right down the bank past the buildings of the former drainage station to follow the path that leads along a dyke away from the river.

Continue south along the dyke past pockets of woodland until reaching a track that leads left into private land

Look for herons around here as a little to the north across the river is Hilgay Heronry.

An old drainage station on the bank of the River Wissey near Hilgay

185

and right alongside another wood. Turn right and follow the track to the end of the wood and, where it meets another track, turn right then left along Sandy Lane, which, as its name suggests, is quite sandy. This passes **Wood Hall** across the field to the left and towards a water tower ahead.

Arriving at a corner with a gatehouse, take the footpath that leads along the edge of a field in the same westerly direction towards the water tower. Follow this right at the corner of the field, then right again at the next corner, before turning sharp left to reach a road. Turn left onto Woodhall Road and follow this past the junction with Hubbard's Drove to the right, and the gateway that leads to the church to the left, to reach Hilgay's High Street by a school and war memorial. Turn right and walk past a shop, village hall and Methodist chapel to return to the walk's starting point at the pub. ◄

Just beyond the Rose & Crown in Hilgay is the main bridge over the River Wissey, which has attractive views in both directions.

Hilgay village sits on the south bank of the River Wissey, a tributary of the Great Ouse, on higher land than most of the surrounding countryside. At the time of the Domesday Book it was an island and one of only two places recorded in the Norfolk fens. The village was famous in Saxon and early Norman times for the large numbers of eels and fish caught here.

The village churchyard is the final resting place of George William Manby (1765–1854), a contemporary of Nelson, who invented a rocket-powered lifeline that could be fired at ships in distress and which is estimated to have saved nearly a thousand lives during his lifetime.

WALK 40
The Wiggenhalls

Start	Wiggenhall St Germans village hall (TF 593 142)
Distance	6 miles (9.6km) or 8½ miles (13.6km) with extension
Time	2hr 20min, 3hr 30min with extension
Map	OS Landranger 131 Boston & Spalding, 143 Ely & Wisbech, Explorer 236 King's Lynn, Downham Market & Swaffham
Refreshments	Pub at Wiggenhall St Germans
Public Transport	Hourly bus service to both Wiggenhalls from King's Lynn
Parking	Village hall car park, Wiggenhall St Germans

A riverside walk deep in the Fenland country of west Norfolk that has some of the best that this landscape has to offer – isolated waterside villages, appealing historic churches, vast channels of water and enormous skies. A section of this walk follows part of the Fen Rivers Way, a long distance path between Cambridge and King's Lynn that follows the banks of the Cam and River Great Ouses.

Starting at the village hall, cross the road to walk down Sluice Road past council houses. Follow the road as it bends right over a sluice then left past St Germans Pumping Station and over **St Mary's Bridge,** spanning Middle Level Main Drain. Continue past houses on both sides to reach a junction and turn sharp right along Church Lane. Pass the Primitive Methodist Chapel towards the church tower ahead and follow the road left, right then left again at the footpath along the drive of a house to reach **St Mary the Virgin Church.** ▸

The key to St Mary the Virgin Church is available at the house by the entrance drive.

St Mary the Virgin Church gives its name to the village of Wiggenhall St Mary the Virgin, one of four Wiggenhalls on or close to the River Ouse. The church of St Mary the Virgin has an attractive sundial dated 1742 above its porch that bears the legend: 'Joseph Rockley, Church Warden – Tempus Fugit'. The church also has one of the best collections of

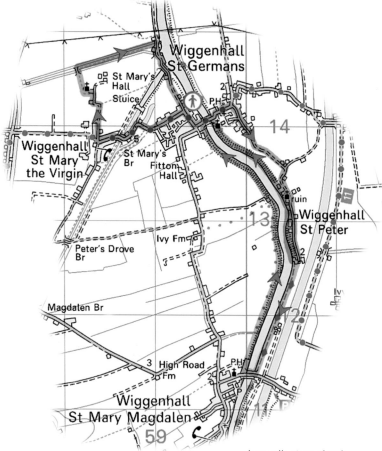

best collections of 15th and 16th century benches in the county, with carved bench ends that depict a variety of saints, animals and figures in Tudor dress. Other fine bench ends may be seen at St Germain Church at Wiggenhall St Germans across the river.

Leave the churchyard at its northwest corner and take the path that leads right along a field edge. Crossing the field, the buildings of **St Mary's Hall** become visible through trees to the right. Meeting two parallel water channels, cross a small bridge over Mill Basin, the first of the channels, then turn right to walk along the raised bank between the channels. ▶ Follow the central track to reach another bridge and a house. Go to the left of the house and walk up to the road. Cross over the road and head right along the raised bank of the River Great Ouse, briefly returning to the road when necessary to cross over channels. St Germain Church and the road bridge over the river lie straight ahead. Return to the road to pass Eau Brink Pumping Station before returning to the bank again to walk past houses and along a low wall to reach the road bridge.

To the left, beyond power lines, the factories at King's Lynn's outskirts can be clearly seen in the distance.

The **River Great Ouse** is the fourth longest river in the United Kingdom, running 143 miles (229km) from its source close to Wappenham in Northamptonshire to The Wash at King's Lynn. The river's course has been greatly altered through time

The River Great Ouse, looking north to Wiggenhall St Germans

due to the construction of various drainage and navigational channels in The Fens since the region was first drained in the early 17th century. It was the diversion of the river to King's Lynn that allowed the Norfolk town to develop as a port shipping farm produce from the fertile, newly drained fens.

Turn left over the bridge, then continue straight on with the **pub** and church on your right. Go past a chapel and turn right at the road junction along St Peter's Road. Follow this road south out of the village, the raised bank of the Great Ouse never going out of sight to the right. At a junction next to a couple of isolated houses, take the road to the right that leads towards St Peter Church. This passes another group of houses and paddocks before passing the semi-ruined St Peter Church on the right. Continue past more houses to the very end of the road and, where it stops at the last of the houses, go through a gate to walk up to the bank of the river. ◀ If not continuing to **Wiggenhall St Mary Magdalen**, turn right to walk along the river bank back in the direction of **Wiggenhall St Germans**, passing St Peter Church along the way. Once back at the bridge, turn left across the river then right along School Road to return to the village hall and starting point.

At this point there is the option of extending the walk by continuing south to the bridge at Wiggenhall St Mary Magdalen and returning on the opposite bank.

APPENDIX A

Route summary table

Walk	Start/Finish	Distance	Time	Page
1 Winterton-on-Sea	Beach car park, Winterton-on-Sea (TG 498 198)	5 miles (8km)	2hr	27
2 Potter Heigham and Hickling Broad	Medieval bridge, Potter Heigham (TG 420 185)	5½ miles (8.8km)	2hr 15min	31
3 North Walsham	North Walsham Market Cross (TG 282 303)	8 miles (12.8km)	3hr	35
4 Happisburgh	Happisburgh beach car park (TG 385 308)	4½ miles (7.2km)	1hr 50 min	39
5 Horstead and River Bure	Recruiting Sergeant pub, Horstead (TG 264 196)	4½ miles (7.2km)	2hr	42
6 River Chet and Hardley Marshes	White Horse Inn, Chedgrave (TG 361 992)	8 miles (12.8km)	3hr 15 min	47
7 Outney Common and Earsham	Bungay Castle, Suffolk (TM 335 898)	5½ miles (8.8km)	2hr 15min	50
8 Rockland St Mary and Claxton	Rockland Broad staithe (TG 328 047)	6½ miles (10.4km)	2hr 45min	54
9 Surlingham	Surlingham St Mary's Church (TG 305 065)	4½ miles (7.2km)	1hr 45min	58

Walk		Start/Finish	Distance	Time	Page
10	Burgh St Peter and 'The Triangle'	Burgh St Peter village hall (TM 468 935)	6 miles (9.6km)	2hr 15min	62
11	Burgh Castle	Queens Head pub, Burgh Castle (TG 481 052)	4½ miles (7.2km)	2hr	66
12	Shotesham	Shotesham All Saints Church (TM 246 990)	7½ miles (12km)	3hr	70
13	Fritton Common	Fritton Common (TM 225 927)	4 miles (6.4km)	1hr 30min	73
14	Harleston and Redenhall	Harleston Market Place (TM 245 833)	6½ miles (10.4km)	2hr 30min	76
15	Cringleford and River Yare	Car park near Cringleford Bridge on Newmarket Road (TG 021 061)	4½ miles (7.2km)	2hr	80
16	New and Old Buckenham	St Martin Church, New Buckenham (TL 088 906)	4½ miles (7.2km)	2hr	84
17	Sheringham and Beeston Regis	Sheringham seafront (TG 158 436)	5 miles (8km)	2hr	89
18	Bodham and Baconsthorpe	Bodham village hall (TG 126 402)	7½ miles (12km)	3hr	94
19	Itteringham	Bure Valley Community Centre, Itteringham (TG 145 309)	5 miles (8km)	2hr	98
20	Aylsham and Blickling	Aylsham Market Place (TG 193 270)	7 miles (11.2km)	2hr 45 min	101
21	Old Hunstanton, Thornham and Holme-next-the-Sea	Le Strange Arms Hotel, Old Hunstanton (TF 679 424)	12 miles (19.2km)	4hr 45min	105

Walk		Start/Finish	Distance	Time	Page
22	Snettisham	Snettisham, Rose & Crown pub (TF 686 343)	7 miles (11.2km)	2hr 45min	111
23	Salthouse and Cley-next-the-Sea	Salthouse, The Green (TG 074 439)	8 miles (12.8km)	3hr 20min	115
24	Blakeney and Wiveton Downs	Blakeney Quay (TG 028 442)	5 or 6¼ miles (8 or 10km)	2hr – 2hr 30min	120
25	Little Walsingham, Houghton St Giles and Great Snoring	Coker's Hill Car Park, Little Walsingham (TF 933 369)	7 miles (11.2km)	3hr	124
26	Brancaster Staithe and Barrow Common	Jolly Sailors pub, Brancaster Staithe (TF 793 443)	4½ miles (7.2km)	1hr 50min	129
27	Thompson Common and Pingo Trail	Car park just off A1075 between Watton and Thetford (TL 941 966)	7½ miles (12km)	3hr 15min	134
28	Swannington and Upgate Common	St Margaret Church, Swannington (TG 134 193)	4 miles (6.4km)	1hr 45min	138
29	Hockering	Victoria pub, Hockering (TG 073 130)	5 miles (8km)	2hr	141
30	Shipdham	Shipdham All Saints Church (TF 958 074)	4½ miles (7.2km)	1hr 45min	145
31	Santon Warren and Thetford Forest	Santon Downham Forestry Office (TL 816 878)	7 miles (11.2km)	3hr	148
32	Harpley and Peddars Way	Rose and Crown pub, Harpley (TF 788 258)	7½ miles (11.2km)	3hr	154

Walk		Start/Finish	Distance	Time	Page
33	Tittleshall and Godwick	St Mary's Church, Tittleshall (TF 894 211)	4½ miles (7.2km)	2hr	158
34	Helhoughton and West Raynham	All Saints Church, Helhoughton (TF 869 265)	4 miles (6.4km)	1hr 45min	163
35	Castle Acre	Ostrich pub, Castle Acre (TF 816 152)	7½ miles (12km)	3hr	167
36	Roydon and Roydon Common	Three Horseshoes pub, Roydon (TF 707 228)	7 miles (11.2km)	2hr 30min	171
37	Narborough and Nar Valley	All Saints Church, Narborough (TF 747 130)	8 miles (12.8km)	3hr	174
38	Beachamwell	The Green, Beachamwell (TF 751 053)	7 miles (11.2km)	2hr 45min	179
39	Hilgay Fen	Rose & Crown pub, Hilgay (TL 621 987)	4 miles (6.4km)	1hr 40min	184
40	The Wiggenhalls	Wiggenhall St Germans village hall (TF 593 142)	6 miles (9.6km) or 8½ miles (13.6km) with extension	2hr 20min – 3hr 30min	187

APPENDIX B
Useful contacts

Visit Norfolk
www.visitnorfolk.co.uk

Visit North Norfolk
www.visitnorthnorfolk.co.uk

Visit West Norfolk
www.visitwestnorfolk.com

Norfolk Coast Partnership
www.norfolkcoastaonb.org.uk

Enjoy the Broads
www.enjoythebroads.com

Brecks Partnership
www.brecks.org

Peddars Way/Norfolk Coast Path
www.nationaltrail.co.uk/
peddars-way-and-norfolk-coast-path

Long Distance Walkers Association
www.ldwa.org.uk

Norfolk Wildlife Trust
www.norfolkwildlifetrust.org.uk

Traveline East Anglia
www.travelineeastanglia.org.uk

Norfolk Tourist Information
www.norfolktouristinformation.com

Tourist Information Centres
Norwich
The Forum
Millennium Plain
Norwich NR2 1TF
Tel: 01603 213999
www.visitnorfolk.co.uk

Broads Authority Visitor Centre
Whitlingham Country Park
Whitlingham Lane Trowse
Norwich
NR14 8TR
Tel: 01603 756094
www.broads-authority.gov.uk

Great Yarmouth
Maritime House
25 Marine Parade
Great Yarmouth NR30 2EN
Tel: 01493 846346
www.great-yarmouth.co.uk

North Walsham
Information Office
Council Offices
New Road
North Walsham NR28 9DE
Tel: 01692 404114
www.northwalsham-town.co.uk

Loddon
The Old Town Hall
1 Bridge Street
Loddon NR14 6LZ
Tel: 01508 521028
www.south-norfolk.gov.uk

Diss
Meres Mouth
Mere Street
Diss IP22 4AG
Tel: 01379 650523

Wymondham
Market Cross
Market Place
Wymondham NR18 0AX
Tel: 01953 604721

Thetford
20 King Street
Thetford IP24 2AP
Tel: 01842 751975
www.leapinghare.org

Swaffham
Town Museum
4 London Street
Swaffham PE37 7DQ
www.aroundswaffham.co.uk

Cromer
North Norfolk Information Centre
Louden Road
Cromer NR27 9EF
Tel: 01263 512497
www.north-norfolk.gov.uk

Sheringham
Station Approach
Sheringham NR26 8RA
Tel: 01263 824329
www.north-norfolk.gov.uk

Aylsham
Bure Valley Railway Station
Norwich Road
Aylsham NR11 6BW
Tel: 01263 733903
www.broadland.gov.uk

Holt
3 Pound Close
Market Place
Holt NR25 6BW
Tel: 01263 713100
www.north-norfolk.gov.uk

Wells-next-the-Sea
Staithe Street
Wells-next-the-Sea NR23 1AN
Tel: 01328 710885
www.north-norfolk.gov.uk

Walsingham
Shire Hall Museum
Little Walsingham NR27 1YQ
Tel: 01328 820510
www.north-norfolk.gov.uk

Burnham Deepdale
Deepdale Visitor Information Centre
Deepdale Backpackers & Camping
Main Road
Burnham Deepdale PE31 8DD
Tel: 01485 210256
www.deepdalebackpackers.co.uk

Hunstanton
Town Hall
The Green
Hunstanton PE36 6BQ
Tel: 01485 532610
www.visithunstanton.info

King's Lynn
The Custom House
Purfleet Quay
King's Lynn PE30 1HP
Tel: 01553 763044
www.west-norfolk.gov.uk

Downham Market
The Priory Centre
78 Priory Road
Downham Market PE38 9JS
Tel: 01553 763044
www.visitwestnorfolk.com

APPENDIX C

Further reading

P Brooks, *The Norfolk Almanac of Disasters* (DB Publishing)

G R Dunn, *North Norfolk, a Landscape Guide* (Limestone Publishing)

D Dymond, *The Norfolk Landscape* (Alastair Press)

J Gibbs, *The Broads: Waterways of Norfolk and Suffolk* (Frances Lincoln)

J Gibbs, *The Norfolk Coast* (Frances Lincoln)

N Glenn, *Best Birdwatching Sites in Norfolk* (Buckingham Press)

N Holmes, *The Lawless Coast: Murder, Smuggling and Anarchy in the 1780s on the North Norfolk Coast* (The Larks Press)

R Malster, *The Norfolk and Suffolk Broads* (The History Press)

F Meeres, *North Norfolk Coast* (Phillimore & Co Ltd)

L Mitchell, *Slow Travel Norfolk*(Bradt)

D P Mortlock and C V Roberts, *Guide to Norfolk Churches* (Lutterworth Press)

M Rice, *Building Norfolk* (Frances Lincoln)

D Stanford, *Norfolk Churches* (Frances Lincoln)

N R Storey, *The Little Book of Norfolk* (The History Press)

N R Storey, *The Lost Coast of Norfolk* (The History Press)

S Wade Martins, *History of Norfolk* (Phillimore & Co Ltd)

APPENDIX D
Long distance walks in Norfolk

The 46-mile (74km) **Peddars Way**, which links with the Norfolk Coast Path at Holme-next-the-Sea, is Norfolk's principal long distance footpath. It starts at Knettishall Heath in Suffolk, where it also links with the Angle's Way.

The **Norfolk Coast Path** is a 45-mile (72km) long distance route between Hunstanton and Cromer that links with the Peddars Way at Holme-next-the-Sea.

Angles Way is a 93-mile (149km) long distance path shared with Suffolk that runs along the Waveney and Little Ouse rivers between Great Yarmouth and Thetford in the Norfolk Brecks.

Wherryman's Way is a 35-mile (56km) recreational route that runs from Norwich to the coast at Great Yarmouth largely along the banks of the River Yare.

Weavers' Way is a 59-mile (95km) long distance footpath linking Cromer, Aylsham, North Walsham, the Broads and Great Yarmouth.

Boudica's Way (or **Boudicca Way**) is a 36-mile (58km) long distance footpath that runs through south Norfolk between Norwich and Diss.

Iceni Way is an 83-mile (134km) long distance footpath from Knettishall Heath to Hunstanton via valleys of the Little Ouse and River Great Ouses. The route includes the Little Ouse Path and part of the Fen Rivers Way.

Tas Valley Way is a 25-mile (40km) long distance path between Norwich and Attleborough in south Norfolk.

Nar Valley Way is a 34 mile (54km) long distance path entirely within the watershed of the River Nar between King's Lynn and Gressenhall near East Dereham.

Fen Rivers Way is a 50-mile (80km) long distance path between Cambridge and King's Lynn that follows the banks of the Cam and River Great Ouses and passes through both Cambridgeshire and Norfolk.

Wensum Way is a new 12-mile (20km) route linking Nar Valley way and marriot's Way, enabling a cross-Norfolk route bwteen King's Lynn and Great Yarmough.

Peter Scott Walk is a ten-mile (16km) walk along the coast of the Wash from the mouth of the River Nene to the ferry crossing to King's Lynn on the River Great Ouse.

Paston Way is a meandering 18-mile (29km) route between Cromer and North Walsham that takes in a number of parish churches along the way.

Kett's Country is a 17-mile (27km) recreational route between Norwich and Wymondham.

Marriotts Way, which follows the 22-mile (36km) route of the old Norwich–Aylsham railway, is a combined walking/cycling route.

The Little Ouse Path follows the Little Ouse River for ten miles (16km) through Thetford Forest in both Norfolk and Suffolk.

The following long distance walks also pass through Norfolk but are mostly outside the county:
Hereward Way, **Icknield Way Path**, **Ouse Valley Way** and **St Edmund Way**.

NOTES

NOTES

NOTES

NOTES

LISTING OF CICERONE GUIDES

For full information on all our
guides, books and eBooks, visit our
website: **www.cicerone.co.uk**